D1602519

Speaking of
Sex

Speaking of Sex

FUNNY, WICKED & JOYFUL REMARKS ABOUT ALMOST EVERYBODY'S FAVORITE SUBJECT

John-Paul Sousa

Copyright © 2002 by John-Paul Sousa.

ISBN: Softcover   1-4010-4739-4

All rights reserved. No part of this book may be reproduced or
transmitted in any form or by any means, electronic or mechanical,
including photocopying, recording, or by any information storage
and retrieval system, without permission in writing from the
copyright owner.

This book was printed in the United States of America.

To order additional copies of this book, contact:
Xlibris Corporation
1-888-795-4274
www.Xlibris.com
Orders@Xlibris.com
14483

From their lips
to your ears . . .

Anonymous
"Sex is nobody's business except the three people
involved."

Steve Martin
"I believe that sex is the most beautiful, natural,
and wholesome thing that money can buy."

Sally Struthers
"If a man is pictured chopping off a woman's
breast, it only gets an 'R' rating. But if, God forbid,
a man is pictured kissing a woman's breast it gets
an 'X' rating. Why is violence more acceptable
than tenderness?"

Roger Crew
"What part of 'Aww c'mon, please?' don't you
understand?"

Cynthia Heimel
"Get your tongue out of my mouth, I'm kissing you
goodbye."

Read it aloud or under the covers. It's a sure delight!

Contents

ACKNOWLEDGEMENTS

Thanks to the witty, perverse and profound people whose comments make up this book. If you have any sex quotes you'd like to see in future editions, please e-mail them to: speakingofsex@excite.com.

INTRODUCTION

Say what you will about sex, but nothing creates as much controversy. You'd think we'd have gotten used to it by now.

For better *and* worse, we haven't. Sex still retains its wonderful charms that inspire, comfort and delight. It has a unique ability to focus our attention on the present moment. In the throes of sexual pleasure we're fully alive. Stresses and mundane existence fall away as we're lifted by tidal waves of bliss.

But for all of us who are living passionate lives there are others who say, now wait a minute, you've got to draw the line somewhere. And it's extremely revealing where people draw that line. It provides invaluable insight into their true nature.

United States Attorney General John Ashcroft, for example, in early 2002 ordered $8,000 worth of blue drapes for the purpose of concealing two classical statues that have stood in the Great Hall of the Justice Department since the 1930s. Ashcroft, in his flat, curt Midwestern voice, said he felt "uncomfortable" being photographed in front of the gleaming aluminum sculptures: a female "Spirit of Justice" with one breast exposed and one covered by a Grecian tunic, and her male counterpart, the "Majesty of Justice," clothed in a loincloth.

After strong reactions against the cover-up surfaced in the media, Ashcroft reportedly advised his staff to cite "aesthetic reasons" for adding the blue drapes. A curious rationale, since the now hidden statues are featured in fine arts guidebooks to the Washington, D.C. area.

If the statues are no longer visible, the chilling symbolism is: the Spirit of Justice has been officially replaced by the Spirit of Repression.

Of course, this behavior isn't limited to any one place or administration. Listen to how we talk about sex. Watch how we portray it. All too often the context is criminal, clinical, sensational — everything but natural.

When a father in Indiana recently filed a lawsuit to force his daughter's school bus to change it route so it wouldn't pass a replica of Michelangelo's statue of David, he probably intended to "protect" his daughter from the view itself or from the snickers of some immature boys on the bus — perhaps both. The statue is nude, after all, a fact which seems to distort all other facts, including that it's an artistic masterpiece revered for centuries around the world. It's been viewed by millions of men, women and children. A few may have giggled, many were probably inspired, but there are no reports of anyone being harmed by viewing the statue.

When Michelangelo's David and partially nude statues at the Justice Department still sound alarms and boil the blood in America today, we're clearly a culture that's frightened by our own bodies — and by extension, human affection.

Missed opportunities like these happen in communities across the country every week. We plant seeds of shame and ignorance, then reap a bitter crop: alienation from our own bodies. And if alienation is how we live, then alienation is what we teach.

Maybe this explains why (amazingly!) most of what's labeled "sex" in news reports, films and lawsuits is far removed from the sex act itself. Anything with a trace of sexuality or sensuality becomes suspect.

By restricting open and honest expressions of sexuality, we've become a nation that approaches sex like adolescents leering through a peephole in the girls' shower. Not great preparation for real relationships with real people.

But it doesn't end there. You see it in the way we keep everyone at arm's length. A study by researcher Helen Colton observed that Parisians, during a normal conversation, make physical contact with the person they're talking to at least 100 times an hour. For Americans, that number drops to four!

We're a culture that adores violence, accepts the ever-widening gap between rich and poor, but is scared to death of affectionate human contact. We swoop down on it with suspicion and gossip, not to mention legal prosecutions. Then we act surprised when these unmet needs fester into loneliness and isolation. It doesn't have to be that way.

Where are the vivid images of positive sexual relationships? Where's the sensual poetry we can bring to daily life?

Sex can do more than shock and sell merchandise. A healthy sexual attitude can rejuvenate the way we see ourselves. It can strengthen our connection with others. It can even reveal a mystical confluence between sexuality and spirituality.

One thing's certain: we won't get there by talking about sex in shameful, hypocritical tones. We need to embrace a new vocabulary that recognizes sex as the life force.

Where to begin?

Laughing about sex seems a good first step toward humanizing it. So in a time and place where everything is taken so damn seriously, *Speaking of Sex* offers you a humorous, joyful, irreverent celebration of men and women and our shared dance of intimacy.

John-Paul Sousa

≈ 1 ≈

Dating: A Job Interview That Lasts All Night

When you're dating, you're basically leasing the pussy with an option to buy.

Eddie Murphy

When a guy says, "Do you want to go to a movie?" what he's really saying is, "I'd eventually like to have sex with you." When a guy says, "Can I call you sometime?" what he's really saying is, "I'd eventually like to have sex with you."

John-Paul Sousa

I'm driving her home, and that's when I start to wonder if there's going to be any sex – and if I'm going to be involved.

Garry Shandling

Would you like to come back to my place and do
what I'm going to tell my friends we did anyway?

Spanky

I drove to the Pleasure Chest and picked up $400 worth
of sex toys and outfits. I had my overnight duffel in one
hand and a shopping bag full of lubricants, vibrating
clitoral stimulators and ben-wa balls in the other. I was
ready to rock her fucking world.

Tommy Lee, on preparing for his first
date with Pamela Anderson

The hard-on is a lonely hunter.

Al Goldstein

If men knew all that women think, they'd be
twenty times more daring.

Alphonse Karr

Dating is more complicated than calculus, more
nerve-wracking than midterms, and more
embarrassing than a gym uniform.

Clarissa Darling, in "Clarissa Explains It All"

We're completely wrong for each other. But that's
not the only attraction.

Woody Allen

A man shall win us best with flattery.

Geoffrey Chaucer, "The Wife of Bath's Tale"

When a boy and girl experience their first kiss,
they find love's oneness, a feeling so strong that

they can no longer see each other's faults. The
kiss is the gateway to bliss and amorous
experience. The kiss provokes erotic ardor,
agitates the heart, and is an incitation to the
natural gift of self.

The Kama Sutra

Romance . . . is rape embellished with meaningful
looks.

Andrea Dworkin

She was a lesbian with doubts about her
masculinity.

Peter DeVries

Never date a woman you can hear ticking.

Mark Patinkin

I must paint you.

Paul Gauguin, pick-up line

Amish pick-up line: Are thee up for some plowing?

David Letterman

Hey, baby, wanna get fucked?

World's worst pick-up line

You got Jordan River in your hips, mama,
Daddy's screaming to be baptized.

J. D. Short, song lyric

Let's Put the "X" in Sex.

Kiss, song title

To succeed with the opposite sex tell her you're impotent. She can't wait to disprove it.

Cary Grant

Why don't you come up sometime, and see me?

Mae West

It's very awkward being a single guy with all the diseases around. It's to the point where I won't go to bed with a woman unless she says, "All right, I'll go to bed with you."

Garry Shandling

There are a number of mechanical devices which increase sexual arousal, particularly in women. Chief among these is the Mercedes-Benz 380SL convertible.

P. J. O'Rourke

Wherever there are rich men trying not to feel old there will be young girls trying not to feel poor.

Julie Burchill

Power. That's what women are drawn to.

Sylvester Stallone

Liquor in the front, poker in the rear.

Bar sign

To get thine ends, lay bashfulness aside;
Who fears to ask, doth teach to be deny'd.

Robert Herrick

. . . the man should seize her delicate waist and
fondle her jade-like body. Talking of being bound
together, with one heart and a single intent, they
should embrace and kiss, suck tongues, press close
and caress each other's ears and head. Soothing
above and stimulating below, the many coquetries
are revealed. Then the woman should take his
Jade Stalk in her left hand, while he strokes her
Jade Gate with his right; moved by the life-force of
the female element, his Jade Stalk becomes
excited; stimulated by the life force of the male
element, her Jade Gate begins to bubble over, like
a stream flowing into a valley.

Taoist Master Tung, 179-104 BCE

A mistress should be like a little country retreat
near the town, not to dwell in constantly, but only
for a night and away.

William Wycherley

The walks over soft grass, the smiles over
candlelight, the arguments over just about
everything else.

Max Headroom

I have often depended on the blindness of
strangers.

Adrienne E. Gusoff

The happiest moment of any affair takes place
after the loved one has learned to accommodate
the lover and before the maddening personality of
either party has emerged like a jagged rock from
the receding tides of lust and curiosity.

Quentin Crisp

Won't you come into the garden? I would like my roses to see you.

Richard Brinsley Sheridan

Seduction is often difficult to distinguish from rape. In seduction, the rapist bothers to buy a bottle of wine.

Andrea Dworkin

Sometimes I look at a cute guy and get a uterus twinge.

Carrie Snow

I am a twenty-three-year-old woman who has been on the pill for two years. It's getting expensive and I think my boyfriend should share half the cost, but I don't know him well enough to discuss money.

Letter to Dear Abby

It can be great fun to have an affair with a bitch.

Louis Auchincloss

Next to the pleasures of taking a new mistress is that of being rid of an old one.

William Wycherley

The desire engendered in the male gland is a hundred times more difficult to control than the desire bred in the female glands. All girls agreeing to a lovers' lane tete-a-tete in a car, knowing that they will limit their actions to arousing desires and then defend their "virtue," should be horsewhipped.

Marlene Dietrich

If you aren't going all the way, why go at all?

Joe Namath

Brisk confidence still best with woman copes:
Pique her and soothe in turn – soon passion
crowns they hopes.

Lord Byron

It's easy to make a friend. What's hard is to make a
stranger.

Anonymous

Said a fussy old bachelor named Harridge:
"Connubial life I disparage.
Every time I get hot
And poke some girl's spot,
She thinks it's an offer of marriage."

Anonymous

Being with a woman all night never hurt no
professional baseball player. It's staying up all night
looking for a woman that does him in.

Casey Stengel

You gotta learn that if you don't get it by midnight,
chances are you ain't gonna get it; and if you do, it
ain't worth it.

Casey Stengel

Raquel Welch asked me out once. I was standing in
her home at the time.

Leonard Barr

Dating is a social engagement with the threat of sex at its conclusion.

P.J. O'Rourke

What is all this dinner-and-a-movie shit? Why can't people just go somewhere and fuck for three or four hours?

George Carlin

I think men talk to women so they can sleep with them and women sleep with men so they can talk to them.

Jay McInerney

Familiarity breeds attempt.

Goodman Ace

Whether a pretty woman grants or withholds her favors, she always likes to be asked for them.

Ovid

The lame tongue gets nothing.

William Camden

The difference between a bachelor girl and a spinster is sex.

Anonymous

Dancing is a perpendicular expression of a horizontal desire.

Anonymous

Women that delight in courting are willing to yield.

John Lyly

Dear Abby:
My boyfriend is going to be twenty-years-old next
month. I'd like to give him something nice for his
birthday. What do you think he'd like?

Carol

Dear Carol:
Never mind what he'd like. Give him a tie.

Abby

I believe in the theory that anyone can get laid, it's
just a matter of lowering your standards enough.

Michael Stipe

You only lie to two people in your life: your
girlfriend and the police.

Jack Nicholson

Girlfriend: Someone who knows everything,
except why she's dating you.

John-Paul Sousa

Never be possessive. If a female lets on that she is
going out with another man, be kind and
understanding. If she says she would like to go out
with all the Dallas Cowboys, including the coaching
staff, the same applies . . . Unless you actually care
about her, in which case you must see to it that she
has no male contact whatsoever.

Bruce Jay Friedman

Being bald is an unfailing sex magnet.

Telly Savalas

Music helps set a romantic mood. Imagine her surprise when you say, "I don't need a stereo – I have an accordion!" Then imagine the sound of the door slamming.

Martin Mull

She was a lovely girl. Our courtship was fast and furious: I was fast and she was furious.

Max Kauffmann

I can understand companionship. I can understand bought sex in the afternoon. I cannot understand the love affair.

Gore Vidal

The follies which a man regrets most in his life are those which he didn't commit when he had the opportunity.

Helen Rowland

Girls, in fact, are always manipulating men: It's called cock-teasing.

Camille Paglia

A promise to a woman is just a lie that hasn't happened yet.

Bobcat Goldthwait

When I'm in a wig I'm pretty attractive. I stare at myself in mirrors because I'm my type.

Kevin McDonald

There is no one, no matter their size, shape, accent, who doesn't turn someone else on, somewhere, somehow.

Larry Levenson

Since nature's first thrust is always toward the physical, it would be contrary to the natural order of things to begin by occupying lovers with transcendent and spiritual illusions. The natural impulses should first be reinforced and then the sentiments should be brought into play.

Charles Fourier

Women go out and say, "Before I go to bed with a man, I want to know who he is as a person." Guys are thinking, "Let's get them in bed before they find out who we are."

Tony Stone

Girls are like problems on a math test. You do all the easy ones first, then if you have time you go back and try the hard ones.

Anonymous

He who begins timidly invites refusal.

Seneca

I scarcely seem to be able to keep my hands off you.

Ovid

You have to penetrate a woman's defenses. Getting into her head is a prerequisite to getting into her body.

Bob Guccione

French is the language that turns dirt into romance.

Stephen King

It is assumed that a woman must wait motionless,
unless she is wooed. That is how the spider waits
for the fly.

George Bernard Shaw

Or if thou think'st I am too quickly won,
I'll frown and be perverse and say thee nay.

William Shakespeare

In choosing a lover you are choosing your destiny.

Mantak Chia

The gander's chasing the goosey
But nobody's goosing me.

Cole Porter, song lyric

I'm dating a woman now who, evidently, is unaware
of it.

Gary Shandling

What part of "Aww c'mon, please?" don't you
understand?

Roger Crew

Let's face it, a date is like a job interview that lasts
all night.

Jerry Seinfeld

꞊2꞊

Masturbation!
The Amazing Availability Of It!

He who hesitates masturbates.

Anonymous

The good thing about masturbation is that you don't have to dress up for it.

Truman Capote

What I like about masturbation is that you don't have to talk afterwards.

Milos Forman

I must have a woman or I shall freeze or turn to stone.

Vincent Van Gogh

Janey got stoned 'cause she couldn't get boned.
                                    Kasey Chambers, song lyric

Boy, was I scared when I first had sex. I was alone at
the time.
                                    Rodney Dangerfield

Just being in a room with myself is almost more
stimulation than I can bear.
                                    Kate Braverman

It would be a lot simpler if there were vending
machines – maybe they could be called Vaginolas –
where for a quarter I could insert my cock, get
vibrated, cum, and then go.
                                    Al Goldstein

A bundle of myrrh is my beloved to me,
That lies all night between my breasts.
                                    Song of Solomon 1:13, The Bible

. . . I pulled out the electric toothbrush to shudder
speedily across my clitoris. Nothing happened. My
vagina packed up and left no forwarding address.
                                    Elise D'Haene

Evil dwells in moist places.
                                    Sister Mary Olivia

It is called in our schools "beastliness," and this is
about the best name for it . . . should it become a
habit it quickly destroys both health and spirits, he
becomes feeble in body and mind, and often ends
in a lunatic asylum.
            Sir Robert Baden-Powell, founder of the Boy Scouts

Masturbation. Don't knock it, it's sex with someone you love.

Woody Allen

The Catholic Church, which refers to masturbation as "self-abuse," is so frightened by man's cock and woman's cunt that all Catholics are generally filled with such horror and self-loathing that they hardly ever manage to function as full human beings.

Al Goldstein

If God had intended us not to masturbate, He would have made our arms shorter.

George Carlin

I was so naive as a kid I used to sneak behind the barn and do nothing.

Johnny Carson

When's the last time you had any poontang?

Dolly Parton

At night, alone, I marry the bed.

Anne Sexton, from "The Ballad of the Lonely Masturbator"

I don't care what your hobby is before puberty hits, but as soon as it does nature gives you a new hobby. Let's just say when I was fourteen I was treated for tennis elbow and I didn't even own a fucking racquet.

Dennis Miller

Masturbation: the primary sexual activity of
mankind. In the 19th century, it was a disease; in
the 20th, it's a cure.

Thomas Szasz

Why,
I said to myself,
with one and a half billion
women in the world,
more or less,
must I lie here
and play night's
silly fluted tune
unaccompanied?

Harry Chapin

I knew nothing at all about sex and simply thought
that masturbation was a unique discovery on my
part.

Jeffrey Bernard

Sexual intercourse is like having someone else
blow your nose.

Philip Larkin

Masturbation: Shaking hands with the unemployed.

George Carlin

The headmaster, who must have been an
enlightened man, summoned all the boys who had
reached the age of puberty to his study and, after
reassuring himself that the door was firmly
secured, made the following brief announcement:
"If you touch it, it will fall off."

Sir Peter Ustinov

The next time you feel the desire coming on,
don't give way to it. If you have the chance, just
wash your parts in cold water and cool them down.

Sir Robert Baden-Powell, to the Boy Scouts

Rehearsal to Ourselves
Of a Withdrawn Delight –

Emily Dickinson

The difference between sex and death is, with
death you can do it alone and nobody's going to
make fun of you.

Woody Allen

Sophisticated persons masturbate without
compunction. They do it for reasons of health,
privacy, thrift, and because of the remarkable
perfection of invisible partners.

P. J. O'Rourke

The woman closed her eyes. Then she held her
arms out as if welcoming someone. She began to
breathe faster and pursed her lips as if she were
kissing someone. Slowly her legs spread and she
squeezed her arms across her large breasts. She was
breathing hard now and almost imperceptibly
began the rhythm of love — back and forth she
went, up and down. Her face was tensing, her body
glistened with perspiration. Then she moaned.
She held her breath, gasped for air. Then for a
long time she just lay there while her breathing
returned to normal. Finally she got up, wiped her
body with a towel and dressed.

Hedy Lamarr, describing
her visit to a Mexican brothel

Masturbation! The amazing availability of it!

James Joyce

≈3≈

I'm As Confident
As Cleopatra's Pussy

If you have a vagina and an attitude in this town,
then that's a lethal combination.

Sharon Stone

Sex appeal is in your heart and head. I'll be sexy
no matter how old or how my body changes.

Sonia Braga

If a woman thinks she's sexy, she is.

Burt Reynolds

I know there are nights when I have power, when I
could put on something and walk in somewhere,
and if there is a man who doesn't look at me, it's
because he's gay.

Kathleen Turner

I have no self-confidence. When a girl tells me yes,
I tell her to think it over.

Rodney Dangerfield

Sex appeal is 50% what you've got and 50% what
people think you've got.

Sophia Loren

I think sexy is more about a state of mind than
what you actually look like.

Lucy Liu

Britney Spears caused controversy last month when
she wore this skimpy outfit at MTV's Video Music
Awards. . . . But I say, ladies, give it up. Britney's ass
looks good. Look at that ass. That is a cherry bomb.
You gotta look at that thing through a hole in a
paper plate. Britney, in about five years that whole
area is gonna blow, so enjoy it now.

Tina Fey

I can't speak for women, but I find Mikhail
Gorbachev attractive as a man's man. It's an
extraordinary combination of intelligence,
baldness and serenity.

Sean Connery

Seamed stockings aren't subtle, but they certainly
do the job. You shouldn't wear them when out
with someone you're not prepared to sleep
with . . . If you really want your escort paralytic with
lust, stop frequently to adjust the seams.

Cynthia Heimel

I've always felt sexy, and I've never had legs.
Confidence is the sexiest thing a woman can have.
It's much sexier than any body part.

Aimee Mullins

The average man is more interested in a woman
who is interested in him than he is in a woman
with beautiful legs.

Marlene Dietrich

All a writer has to do to get a woman is to say he's a
writer. It's an aphrodisiac.

Saul Bellow

There is no aphrodisiac like innocence.

Jean Baudrillard

The only known aphrodisiac is variety.

Marc Connolly

Fame is a powerful aphrodisiac.

Graham Greene

Power is the ultimate aphrodisiac.

Henry Kissinger

I'm as confident as Cleopatra's pussy.

Bette Midler

=4=

Gentlemen Prefer Blondes, But Take What They Can Get

Genitals prefer blondes.

Anonymous

That gentlemen prefer blondes is due to the fact that, apparently, pale hair, delicate skin and an infantile expression represent the very apex of frailty which every man longs to violate.

Alexander King

Of two evils, most men choose the blonde.

Anonymous

Never judge by appearances: the girl who looks like a dumb blonde may really be a smart brunette.

Anonymous

What happens when an irresistible blonde meets an immovable bachelor?

Anonymous

It was a blonde. A blonde to make a bishop kick a hole in a stained glass window.

Raymond Chandler

. . . the artifice of being blonde has some incredible sort of sexual connotation.

Madonna

A chaste woman ought not to dye her hair yellow.

Menander, Greek playwright, 342-291 BC

Blondes have the hottest kisses. Redheads are fair to middling torrid, and brunettes are the frigidest of all. It's something to do with hormones, no doubt.

President Ronald Reagan

Gentlemen prefer blondes, but take what they can get.

Don Herold

=5=

What Men Desire
Is A Virgin Who Is A Whore

I believe that sex is the most beautiful, natural, and wholesome thing that money can buy.

Steve Martin

Men need to be de-spunked regularly. It's when they're not getting a regular de-spunking that they start causing problems. I call that a service, not a nuisance.

Madam Cynthia Payne

If your aim is purity, be a pure bore by day;
When I come home at night, I want a rampant whore.

Martial

When I'm good I'm very good, but when I'm bad
I'm better.

Mae West

That woman can speak eighteen languages and
she can't say "No" in any of them.

Dorothy Parker

I've been in more laps than a napkin.

Mae West

You were born with your legs apart. They'll send
you to your grave in a Y-shaped coffin.

Joe Orton

Oh, the innocent girl
in her maiden teens
knows perfectly well
what everything means.
If she didn't she oughter;
It's a silly shame
to pretend that your daughter
is blank at the game.

D. H. Lawrence

I'm not that innocent.

Britney Spears, song lyric

As the Virgin, woman takes the surrendering role
and man acts as the initiator. She is the "clean slate"
on which he writes the Karmic message, while she
confers and shares her untouchable "pure essence"
with him alone. In this role, she embodies
conventional love at its most potent level. She is the
"pure flower" whose fragrance is his alone to smell.

As the Whore, a woman is in the active role; it is she who acts as the initiatress into the mysteries of love. . . . In this role woman embodies unconventional love. Sure of her sexuality, she offers herself in service without reservation, guilt, or insecurity.

Nik Douglas and Penny Slinger

Clara made love to Gilbert Roland, Victor Fleming, Gary Cooper, John Gilbert, Eddie Cantor, Bela Lugosi, and the entire USC football team.

Daisy DeVoe, Clara Bow's private secretary

'Tisn't beauty, so to speak, nor good talk necessarily. It's just IT. Some women will stay in a man's memory if they once walked down a street.

Rudyard Kipling

In order to avoid being called a flirt, she always yielded easily.

Count Charles Talleyrand

A historical romance is the only kind of book where chastity really counts.

Barbara Cartland

These half-clad girls, to make the men still wilder, used to take me on their laps between dances and kiss and caress and excite me. This was my first impression of the love of women. And you expect me to honor them as you do!

Johannes Brahms

This profession (prostitution) gives me a lot of

freedom. I decide when I start work, when I stop
work, and how much I work.

Stephanie Klee,
asking the German government
to grant sex workers the same rights
as small business owners

Actually, if my business were legitimate, I would
deduct a substantial percentage for depreciation
of my body.

Xaviera Hollander

You'd rather be working at love
Love as your trade

Harry Chapin, song lyric

What do hookers do on their nights off?

Elayne Boosler

I feel like a million tonight – but one at a time.

Mae West

I'd been holding out for so long. I know that
sounds funny to say for someone who was only
thirteen, but I've always been a quick starter.

Ginger Lynn, porn star, on losing her virginity

You are no longer shy
Do it now, I ask you:
Break the membrane of our sweet union.

Saint John of the Cross

My celibacy . . . more a passive habit than an active policy.

John Barth

That man has missed something who has never left a brothel at sunrise feeling like throwing himself into the river out of pure disgust.

Gustave Flaubert

The most romantic thing any woman ever said to me in bed was, "Are you sure you're not a cop?"

Larry Brown

The trouble with a virgin is
She's always on the verge.
A virgin is the worst
Her method is reversed
She'll lead a horse to water
And then let him die of thirst.

E. Y. Harburg

A man can sleep around, no questions asked, but if a woman makes nineteen or twenty mistakes she's a tramp.

Joan Rivers

Girls who put out are tramps. Girls who don't are ladies. This is, however, a rather archaic use of the word. Should one of you boys happen upon a girl who doesn't put out, do not jump to the conclusion that you have found a lady. What you have probably found is a lesbian.

Fran Lebowitz

I wasn't scared, but I still didn't enjoy it at all the
first time. It was like, is this it? Is that all there is?

Taija Rae

Jack and Jill went up the hill
Each with a buck and a quarter.
Jill came down with $2.50.

Andrew Dice Clay

Let him kiss me with the kisses of his mouth –
For your love is better than wine.
. . . Therefore the virgins love you.
Draw me away!

Song of Solomon 1:2-4, The Bible

The difference between sex for money and sex for
free is that sex for money usually turns out to cost a
lot less.

Brendan Behan

When women go bad, men go right after them.

Mae West

"Easy" is an adjective used to describe a woman
who has the sexual morals of a man.

Nancy Linn-Desmond

The woman who has never aroused a man's desire
shouldn't boast of her chastity.

Montaigne

From football player to prostitute: She started as a
tight end, moved to split end, and finished as wide

receiver. Of course, everyone loved her because she never choked on the big ones.

Anonymous

My mother said it was simple to keep a man: you must be a maid in the living-room, a cook in the kitchen, and a whore in the bedroom. I said I'd hire the other two and take care of the bedroom bit.

Jerri Hall

She's the kind of girl who climbed the ladder of success wrong by wrong.

Mae West

The compartment that's easy to put me in is: free-thinking, sexy broad with a dirty mouth, who pretty much does what she wants.

Joan Collins

There goes a good time that was had by all.

Bette Davis

If I still had a cherry, it would have been pushed back so far I could use it for a tail-light.

Nell Kimball

It is fatally easy for Western folk, who have discarded chastity as a value for themselves, to suppose that it can have no value for anyone else.

Germaine Greer

I'll have to marry a virgin. I can't stand criticism.

Isak Dinesen

I've been around so long I knew Doris Day before she was a virgin.

Groucho Marx

She is so pure, Moses couldn't even part her knees.

Joan Rivers, talking about Marie Osmond

Sir Henry Blount was called to the bar for spreading abroad that abominable and dangerous doctrine that it was far cheaper and safer to lie with common wenches than with ladies of quality.

John Aubrey

I never turned over a fig leaf that didn't have a price tag on the other side.

Saul Bellow

A lady is one who never shows her underwear unintentionally.

Lillian Day

Oh, my sister's name is Tilly,
She's a whore in Picadilly,
And my mother is another in The Strand.
And my brother peddles arsehole
At the Elephant and Castle.
We're the finest fucking family in the land.

London street rhyme

Prior to becoming King Edward VII, the Prince of Wales was reportedly arguing with his mistress, Lily Langtry, when he said, "I've spent enough on you to buy a battleship." Her reply was, "And you've spent enough in me to float one."

If all the girls attending the Yale-Harvard game
were laid end to end, I wouldn't be at all surprised.

Dorothy Parker

I thought of losing my virginity as a career move.

Madonna

She's like that old line about justice – not only
must be done, but must be seen to be done.

John Osborne

We may eventually come to realize that chastity is
no more a virtue than malnutrition.

Dr. Alex Comfort

A woman's chastity consists, like an onion, of a
series of coats.

Nathaniel Hawthorne

There is something to be said for whoring: whoring
is according to nature.

John Dennis

The only chaste woman is the one who has not
been asked.

Spanish proverb

My bed has been invaded every night by young
hussies running wild. Yesterday I had three.

Paul Gauguin

Nobody in their right minds would call me a
nymphomaniac. I only sleep with good-looking
men.

Fiona Pitt-Kethley

I used to be Snow White, but I drifted.

Mae West

I'm as pure as the driven slush.

Tallulah Bankhead

Prostitutes are a necessity: without them, men would assault respectable women in the streets.

Napoleon Boneparte

Penal sanctions are not justified for the purpose of attempting to restrain sins against sexual morality committed in private by responsible adults.

J. Dominian

Venus cunningly raised the price of her goods by making pimping illegal.

Montaigne

The best job ever offered to me was to become a landlord in a brothel; it's the perfect milieu for an artist to work in.

William Faulkner

Your idea of fidelity is not having more than one man in bed at the same time.

Frederic Raphael

A bad reputation in a woman allures like the signs of heat in a bitch.

Aldous Huxley

To all you virgins: Thanks for nothing.

John-Paul Sousa

Banish all objects of lust, shut up all youth into the
severest discipline that can be exercised in any
hermitage, ye can not make them chaste . . .

John Milton

This is virgin territory for whorehouses.

Al Capone

I think I have a dick in my brain. I don't need one
between my legs.

Madonna

Chastity is curable, if detected early.

Graffito

Catherine the Great ruled thirty million people
and had three thousand lovers. I do the best I can
in two hours.

Mae West, on her stage role as Catherine

In my country, Australia, we've got legal brothels, a
doctor is in the house, the girls pay taxes, and they
aren't beaten. Prostitution is a part of life.

Rachel Griffiths

Because I can pay her to go away. The others stay
around, want a big romance, movie lovemaking.

Clark Gable, when asked why he used prostitutes

I met only dancing girls . . . all of them devout
students of *Kama Sutra*, which teaches that there
are thirty-nine different postures for the worship
of Dingledangle – the god of love.

*John Barrymore, after a month-long visit to
a Calcutta brothel he called the "Pelvic Palace"*

Prostitution gives her an opportunity to meet
people.

Joseph Heller

Pray, good people, be civil! I am the *Protestant* whore!

Nell Gwynne,
to an angry mob which had mistaken her
for the Catholic mistress of King Charles II of England

She who gapes wide for ten thousand men.

Greek reference to Cleopatra

I like to wake up each morning feeling a new man.

Jean Harlow

What is a promiscuous person? It's usually someone
who is getting more sex than you are.

Victor Lownes

. . . this cooze who's a regular fuck machine. I'm
talking morning, day, night, afternoon . . . dick,
dick, dick.

Quentin Terrantino, from "Reservoir Dogs"

I went down to Piccadilly and picked up a girl who
for a pound was prepared to pass the night with
me. The result was an attack of gonorrhea.
Undeterred by this mishap, however, I continued
whenever I could afford it. There was no romance
in it, no love, only appetite.

Somerset Maugham

. . . I gave her an expensive virgin wool sweater, but her body rejected it.

Rodney Dangerfield

Prostitution seems to be a problem. But what's the problem? Fucking is okay. Selling is okay. So why isn't selling fucking okay?

George Carlin

Well, yeah, I'm a slut.

Jennifer Aniston, from the TV show "Friends"

Some women behave like harlots . . . Therefore I shall deprive them from everlasting life and send them to everlasting death.

Bridget of Sweden, 1303-73

I hate a woman who seems to be hermetically sealed in the lower regions.

Sydney Smith

Musical beds is the faculty sport around here.

Edward Albee

Michael (Jackson) is not interested in girls and sex. He is definitely still a virgin and doesn't believe he has missed anything.

Chris Telvitt, tour manager

I consider promiscuity immoral. Not because sex is evil, but because sex is too good and too important.

Ayn Rand

Good girls go to heaven, bad girls go everywhere.

Anonymous

Whores are the most honest girls. They present the
bill right away.

Alberto Giacometti

Elliot: It doesn't suit women to be promiscuous.
Amanda: It doesn't suit men for women to be
promiscuous.

Noel Coward in "Private Lives"

If a woman hasn't got a tiny streak of a harlot in
her, she's a dry stick as a rule.

D. H. Lawrence

If you want to buy my wares
Follow me and climb the stairs . . .
Love for sale

Cole Porter, song lyric

Romance on short notice was her specialty.

Saki

Aren't women prudes if they don't and prostitutes
if they do?

Kate Millett

I'll wager you that in ten years it will be fashionable
again to be a virgin.

Barbara Cartland

My choice in life was either to be a piano player in
a whorehouse or a politician. And to tell you the
truth, there's hardly any difference.

President Harry S. Truman

She was so exquisite a whore,
That in the belly of her mother
Her cunt was placed so right before,
Her father fucked them both together.

John Wilmot,
Earl of Rochester,
Epitaph on Nell Gwynne

What men desire is a virgin who is a whore.

Edward Dahlberg

₌6₌

Her Lips Suck Forth My Soul

I did not have sexual relations with that woman,
Miss Lewinsky.

President Bill Clinton

Watergate was a crime. Iran-Contra was a crime.
Getting a blowjob is not a crime.

Bill Maher

Only in America could a cocksucker go so far.

Al Goldstein

I regret to say that we of the FBI are powerless to
act in cases of oral-genital intimacy, unless it has in
some way obstructed interstate commerce.

J. Edgar Hoover

Sometimes a cigar is just a cigar.

Sigmund Freud

I think I look quite fetching with those healthy young cocks in my mouth.

Linda Lovelace

She swallowed not only the cock, but all the auxiliary equipment. I couldn't believe she ate the whole thing!

Harry Reems, talking about his sex scene with Linda Lovelace in "Deep Throat"

March isn't the only thing that's in like a lion, out like a lamb.

Anonymous

The red lips open wide,
The slender fingers play their part daintily.
Deep in, deep out; the heart grows wild with passion.
There are no words to tell of the ecstasy that thrills.

The Golden Lotus, a Chinese text, circa 1400

If you are ever in doubt as to whether or not you should kiss a pretty girl, always give her the benefit of the doubt.

Thomas Carlyle

He who hesitates is a damned fool.

Mae West

Sin from my lips? Oh, trespass sweetly urged! Give me my sin again.

William Shakespeare

Kiss me again, kiss me again and again
Give me one of your tastiest kisses
Give me one of your most passionate kisses
And I'll pay you back with four that are hotter than fire.
Louise Labé

I'll let you kiss me sticky.
Gertrude Stein

I kiss the little black forest . . .
Napoleon Boneparte

And down his mouth comes to my mouth! And down
His bright dark eyes come over me, like a hood
Upon my mind! His lips meet mine, and a flood
Of sweet fire sweeps across me, so I drown.
D. H. Lawrence

Each sucks the passion from the other's lips . . . For
stolen joys, in truth, are even the most sweet.
Chin P'ing Mei

Everything tastes more or less like chicken.
Chamberlain's Law

O night beside him!
O tired lips leeching wine,
Achieving honey,
Knowing at last Spring!
A Thousand and One Arabian Nights

The up-dated version of "Little Red Riding Hood"
has the Big Bad Wolf bursting into Grandma's
house and threatening to tear her limb from limb.

"I'll hear nothing of the sort," says Granny. "You'll
eat me like the story says."

Anonymous

You know the worst thing about oral sex? The view.

Maureen Lipman

Feel her body rise
As you kiss her mouth

Sting

What lies lurk in kisses.

Heinrich Heine

Graze on my lips; and if those hills be dry,
Stray lower, where the pleasant fountains lie.

William Shakespeare

Men and women executives should not kiss each
other in public . . . And of course groping is strictly
verboten.

Letitia Baldridge

Whatever the circumstances, open or secret kisses
cause both man and woman wonderful pleasure.
When lovers kiss, their purpose is to draw close to
each other, to develop love and mutual trust.

The Kama Sutra

I want to tell you a terrific story about oral
contraception. I asked this girl to sleep with me
and she said, "No."

Woody Allen

You have to do tobacco like you do women. You
must let it work up to a good chew, let it get moist
and juicy. If you chew too fast, it will become dry
and fall apart.

Phil Garner, baseball player

Any man who'd kiss a woman's bottom, I'd throw
my hat at him. After that he'd kiss anything.

James Joyce

Kiss me, won't you kiss me now
And sleep I would inside your mouth

Dave Matthews, song lyric

A kiss can be a comma, a question mark, or an
exclamation point. That's basic spelling that every
woman ought to know.

Mistinguett

Each kiss a heart-quake, – for a kiss's strength,
I think it must be reckoned by its length.

Lord Byron

Whoever called it necking was a poor judge of
anatomy.

Groucho Marx

Bring your yo-yo,
Wind the string around my tongue.
Mama knows just how to make the yo-yo hum.

Memphis Jug Band

I hate to blow you and run.

Taylor Hayes, porn actress

We kiss and sweat . . .
Tangled tongues and lips

Dave Matthews, song lyric

Get your tongue out of my mouth, I'm kissing you
goodbye.

Cynthia Heimel

If it's uplift you're after, if that's your thrust,
Stop talking, put lips and tongue to other use.

Horace

The languishing eye
Puts in connection soul with soul,
And the tender kiss
Takes the message from member to vulva.

Sheikh Nefzawi

Never do with your hands what you could do better
with your mouth.

Cherry Vanilla

Her lips suck forth my soul.

Christopher Marlowe

꞊7꞊

Making The Beast With Two Backs

You must just acknowledge deep in your heart of hearts that people are supposed to fuck. It is our main purpose in life, all those other activities – playing the trumpet, vacuuming carpets, reading mystery novels, eating chocolate mousse – are just ways of passing time until you can fuck again.

Cynthia Heimel

Sex is nobody's business except the three people involved.

Anonymous

Rowing in Eden
Ah, the Sea!
Might I but moor – Tonight –
In Thee!

Emily Dickinson

Let copulation thrive!

William Shakespeare

... then I asked him with my eyes to ask again yes
and then he asked me would I yes to say yes my
mountain flower and first I put my arms around
him yes and drew him down to me so he could feel
my breasts all perfume yes and his heart was going
like mad and yes I said yes I will Yes.

James Joyce

Sex can be very beautiful. With either sex. Even if
it's with somebody you don't know.

Georgina Spelvin

My breath
          is here
My bones
          are here
My flesh
          is here
I seek you with them
I find you with them

Inuit Indian song

To the lonely it is company; to the forsaken it is a
friend; they that are penniless are yet rich, in that
they still have this majestic diversion.

Caesar

Sex between a man and a woman can be
wonderful – provided you get between the right
man and the right woman.

Woody Allen

There may be some things better than sex, and some things may be worse. But there is nothing exactly like it.

W.C. Fields

Teasing the want –
It – only – can suffice!

Emily Dickinson

I've tried several varieties of sex. The conventional position makes me claustrophobic, and the others give me a stiff neck or lockjaw.

Tallulah Bankhead

Suddenly the door burst open . . . I tried to explain that La Contessa and I were just friends. But it was difficult standing there naked with an erection.

Rodney Dangerfield

Never miss a chance to have sex or appear on television.

Gore Vidal

Too much of a good thing can be wonderful.

Mae West

That was the most fun I ever had without laughing.

Woody Allen

You mean you're not going to fuck me? Look, if you can't fuck me, get me a broomstick! Get me anything. I will fuck anything!

*Viper, on arriving at
a porn agent's office in Los Angeles*

. . . I had the choice of making it with one
hundred fifty people. But I grabbed this
beautiful blonde chick and her husband, and I ate
her for an hour. And then fifteen guys lined up,
and I fucked ten of them . . . But I will say that the
saving factor of the evening was the chick's cunt.

Andrea True,
disco singer and porn star, recalling a party

His frankfurters are oh so sweet
How I like his sausage meat
I can't do without my kitchen man

Oh how that boy can open clams
No one else can touch my hams
I can't do without my kitchen man

When I eat his doughnuts
All I leave is the hole
Anytime he wants to
Why he can use my sugar bowl

Bessie Smith, song lyric

Fornication? But it was in another country, and
besides the wench is dead.

Christopher Marlowe

In America sex is an obsession, in other parts of the
world it is a fact.

Marlene Dietrich

Menage-a-trois is a French phrase. It means "get
out the camcorder."

Anonymous

The guy was about 27-years-old, and it was his first
night out of jail. . . . Maybe it was just a sympathy
fuck. Maybe it was just for kicks. It was horrible. He
fucked like a squirrel, and the whole trailer was
jumping up and down.

Tamara Longley

Seems to me the basic conflict between men and
women, sexually, is that men are like firefighters.
To us, sex is an emergency, and no matter what
we're doing we can be ready in two minutes.
Women, on the other hand, are like fire. They're
very exciting, but the conditions have to be exactly
right for it to occur.

Jerry Seinfeld

Love is not the dying moan of a distant violin, it's
the triumphant twang of a bedspring.

S.J. Perelman

A total orgasm of the body and mind might be
described as a showering of nectar from the head,
running down your insides like a springtime
shower. It is unmistakable, a wave of subtle chi
energy that opens up hidden powers of feeling.
You feel like a newborn baby, only adult and
conscious.

Mantak Chia

Men spend nine months trying to get out of the
womb and the rest of their lives trying to get back
inside.

Anonymous

The orgasm has replaced the Cross as the focus of longing and the image of fulfillment.

Malcolm Muggeridge

When I get that feeling
It's a sexual healing

Marvin Gaye, song lyric

I don't mind where people make love, so long as they don't do it in the street and frighten the horses.

Mrs. Patrick Campbell

Copulation was, I'm sure, Marilyn Monroe's uncomplicated way of saying thank you.

Nunnally Johnson

Is sex dirty? Only if it's done right.

Woody Allen

The only unnatural sex act is that which you cannot perform.

Alfred Kinsey, sex researcher

I don't see so much of Alfred anymore since he got interested in sex.

Mrs. Alfred Kinsey

In olden days a glimpse of stocking
Was looked on as something shocking
Now heaven knows
Anything goes!

Cole Porter, song lyric

Inanna: "Who will plough my vulva?"
Dumuzi: "Great Lady, the king will plough your vulva.
I, Dumuzi the King, will plough your vulva."
Inanna: "Then plough my vulva, man of my heart!
Plough my vulva!"
Ancient Sumerian manuscript, c.4000-c.2000 BC

Do not dig a canal, let me be your canal,
Do not plough a field, let me be your field,
Farmer, do not search for a wet place,
Let me be your wet place!
Ancient Babylonian song

Sex is an emotion in motion.
Mae West

We are dreaming of sex . . . of huge thighs
opening to us like this night.
Kathy Acker

. . . it is her pleasure while being boffed to have
one or the other of my forefingers lodged snugly
up her anus.
Philip Roth

I wish I had invented sex. Sex is #1.
Brigitte Bardot

Sex hasn't been the same since women started
enjoying it.
Lewis Grizzard

Money, it turned out, was exactly like sex. You
thought of nothing else if you didn't have it and
thought of other things if you did.
James Baldwin

You brush it, till I grow aware
Who wants me, and wide ope I burst.

Robert Browning

Sex has to be behind locked doors. If what you're
doing can be done out in the open, you may as
well be pitching horseshoes.

George Burns

When I make love to a girl she scratches, she
screams. Then she realizes I'm not going to take
no for an answer.

Rodney Dangerfield

License my roving hands, and let them go
Before, behind, between, above, below

John Donne

I get very sexually excited on stage. It's like making
love to 9,000 people at once.

Prince

There is a tendency to think of sex as something
degrading; it is not, it is magnificent, an enormous
privilege.

Francis Devas

Like a great storm
the two of us shake
the tree of life
down to the most hidden
fibers of its roots.

Pablo Neruda

I may not be the greatest actress but I've become
the greatest at screen orgasms. Ten seconds of
heavy breathing, roll your head from side to side,
simulate a slight asthma attack and die a little.

Candice Bergen

There are but these things in the world –
Thy mouth of fire,
Thy breasts, thy hands, thy hair upcurled,
And my desire!

Theodore Wratislaw

Now, I always thought that saying "too much sex" is
like saying "too much Christmas."

Tim Meadows

Some people like sex more than others –
You seem to like it a lot.
There's nothing wrong with being
Innocent or high-minded,
But I'm glad you're not.

Wendy Cope

The only way to resolve a situation with a girl is to
jump on her and things will work out.

Lee Marvin

. . . before D.H. Lawrence, Dr. Maugham
(obstetrician) knew that women, given a fraction
of a chance, liked sex as much as men did. When
he said so, he was called a misogynist.

Gore Vidal

i want you to teach me
the warmth of your breath

the weight of your body
i want to experience
the trembles heat
sweatfireiceconvulsionsgasps
thrustsspasmscaressescriesscreams
          until . . .
i

          can   barely
               breathe

educate me with your
mouth tongue shoulders arms fingers
chest hips thighs legs feet toes

Michelle Renee Pichon

They made love as though they were an
endangered species.

Peter DeVries

I'm a big star and I can't even get laid.

Janis Joplin

It is ten times more pleasant to make love during
the day than at night. The particular attraction lies
in being able to behold the other's nakedness, for
such a sight increases desire.

Jou Pu Tuan

I flung closer to his breast,
As sword that, after battle, flings to sheathe;
And, in that hurtle of united souls,
The mystic motions which in common moods
Are shut beyond our sense, broke in on us,
And, as we sate, we felt the old earth spin,
And all the starry turbulence of worlds

Swing round us in their audient circles, till
If that same golden moon were overhead
Or if beneath our feet, we did not know.
> *Elizabeth Barrett Browning*

I'd like to do a love scene with him just to see what
all the yelling is about.
> *Shirley Maclaine, speaking about*
> *her brother Warren Beatty*

Are you going to come quietly, or do I have to use
earplugs?
> *Peter Sellars*

Copulate with them!
Eat their vulvas!
Ejaculate into them!
Make them wet!
> *Australian Aborigine love chant*

Oh, not at all, just a straight-away pounder.
> *Lily Langtry, when asked if*
> *the Prince of Wales was romantic in bed*

Sexual intercourse is kicking death in the ass while
singing.
> *Charles Bukowski*

O night that was my guide,
O night more friendly than the dawn!
O tender night that tied
lover and the loved one,
loved one in the lover fused as one!
> *St. John of the Cross*

If our elaborate and dominating bodies are given us to be denied at every turn, if our nature is always wrong and wicked, how ineffectual we are — like fishes not meant to swim.

Cyril Connolly

I like making love myself and I can make love for about three minutes. Three minutes of serious fucking and I need eight hours sleep and a bowl of Wheaties.

Richard Pryor

When two people make love, there are at least four people present — the two who are actually there and the two they are thinking about.

Sigmund Freud

(In Freudian theory) the brain is viewed as an appendage of the genital glands.

Carl Jung

... the only hope of our ever getting a really beautiful and vigorous and charming civilization is to allow all the world to fuck and bugger and abuse themselves in public and generally misbehave to their heart's content.

Lytton Strachey

This sort of thing may be tolerated by the French — but we are British, thank God.

Viscount Montgomery

No, no, I'll never farm your bed
Nor your smock-tenant be.

Aphra Behn

He said it was artificial respiration but now I find
I'm to have his child.

Anthony Burgess

Contraceptives should be used on every
conceivable occasion.

Spike Milligan

There are only two guidelines in good sex: Don't
do anything you don't really enjoy, and find out
your partner's needs and don't balk them if you
can help it.

Dr. Alex Comfort

The reason people sweat is so they won't catch fire
when making love.

Don Rose

I once made love for an hour and fifteen minutes,
but it was on the night the clocks are set ahead.

Garry Shandling

It has to be admitted that we English have sex on
the brain, which is a very unsatisfactory place to
have it.

Malcolm Muggeridge

If I had as many love affairs as you have given me
credit for, I would now be speaking to you from a
jar in the Harvard Medical School.

Frank Sinatra

We have no right to boast of despising and
combating carnal pleasure, if we cannot feel it, if

we know nothing of it, of its charms and power,
and its most alluring beauties.

Montaigne

Folks, I'm telling you
birthing is hard
and dying is mean —
so get yourself
a little loving
in between.

Langston Hughes

Sexual gratification culminates in full orgasm of
both partners with the friendliness and mutual
feeling of intimacy that always results from the
complete abandonment of self-assertiveness; where
virile pride and feminine passivity are thrown
overboard without any attempt to do so.

Moshe Feldenkrais

Sex in France is a comedy; in England it is a
tragedy; in America it's a melodrama; in Italy it's an
opera; in Germany, a reason to take up philosophy.

Anonymous

My music is supposed to make you wanna fuck.

Janis Joplin

Love-making is such a nonverbal thing . . . You can
only say, "he stuck it in her" so many ways.

Colleen McCullough

Two minutes with Venus, two years with mercury.

Dr. J. Earle Moore

Sex has become one of the most discussed subjects of modern times. The Victorians pretended it did not exist; the moderns pretend that nothing else exists.

Bishop Fulton J. Sheen

(Sex is) the thing that takes up the least amount of time and causes the most amount of trouble . . .

John Barrymore

Bed is the poor man's opera.

Italian proverb

Sex: the Tabasco sauce which an adolescent national palate sprinkles on every course in the menu.

Mary D. Winn

What is lust, adult lust, after all, but the desire to recapture the heady sensations of adolescent sexuality?

William Boyd

All this talk about sex, all this worry about sex – big deal. The sun makes me happy. I eat a good fish, he makes me happy. I sleep with a good man, he makes me happy.

Melina Mercouri

(Sex is) the last important human activity not subject to taxation . . .

Russell Baker

Sex: A clever imitation of love. It has all of the action but none of the plot.

William Rotsler

In the movies, sex is romantic and passionate. In real life, sex is often sticky and smelly.

Anonymous

Sex is funny!

Cynthia Heimel

What is an orgasm, except laughter of the loins?

Mickey Rooney

I always thought music was more important than sex. Then I thought if I don't hear a concert for a year-and-a-half it doesn't bother me.

Jackie Mason

People are going to be fornicating when the earth shatters. Good for them.

Robyn Hitchcock

Business is like sex; when it's good, it's very, very good; when it's not so good, it's still good.

Economist Mervyn A. King

Sex is like money; only too much is enough.

John Updike

Finding the cool satisfaction of heaven in the heated embers of the pit.

Warren Goldberg

I haven't been fucked like that since grade school.

Helena Bonham Carter

Sex is the great amateur art.

David Cort

To err is human, but it feels divine.

Mae West

Many a fair nymph has in a cave been spread,
And much good love without a feather bed.

Juvenal

The bed is where lascivious toyings meet,
There use all tricks, and shed shame underneath.

Ovid

The difference between sex and love is that sex
relieves tension and love causes it.

Woody Allen

Sex is one instinct of man which can still make us
experience a kind of near-mystical ecstasy.

Trailok Chandra Majupuria

Sex is making a fool of yourself, exposing yourself
as an asshole. That is why sex is so intimate. Making
mistakes is one of the most revealing and intimate
moments of sexual communication.

Jerry Rubin and Mimi Leonard

Anal sex: A stick in the mud.

Anonymous

Sensual sex. You know that stuff where the woman
spends the whole time trying to cum, but can't –
and the man spends the whole time trying to stop
himself cumming, but can't.

Hanif Kureishi

This is a song about the conflict between desires
of the flesh and spiritual ecstasy. It's about
temptation. Who out there hasn't been
tempted? I gotta have it! I want it! Where did all
this conflict begin? Well, it began in the
beginning in a place called the Garden of
Eden . . . In the Garden of Eden there wasn't no
sin and there wasn't no sex either. Man lived in
a state of innocence. And when it comes to no
sex, I prefer the state of guilt.

Bruce Springsteen

Hear the sound of their buttocks, the men moving
  their penises
For these beautiful girls of the western tribes
And the penis becomes erect as their buttocks move
. . . Semen flowing from them into the young girls
For they are always there, moving their buttocks.
They are always there at the wide expanse of water
Ejaculating among the cabbage palm foliage.

Australian Aborigine Chant

I think I made his back feel better.

*Marilyn Monroe, after meeting
with President John F. Kennedy*

Sex without love is an empty experience. But as
empty experiences go, it's one of the best.

Woody Allen

Sex is one of the nine reasons for reincarnation.
The other eight are unimportant.

Henry Miller

I didn't know how babies were made until I was pregnant with my fourth child.

Loretta Lynn

Shove it in gently but enter deep
Then move it real slow
Move it slowly, slowly,
So that her body is not harmed.

Ancient Lett song

To be human is to be fucked.

Murray Schisgal

Sex isn't everything. But then, what is?

Anonymous

Nothing risqué, nothing gained.

Alexander Woollcott

Sex is the greatest thing in life. It cannot be left out of account. We ourselves are but expressions of it.

John S. Bayne

Why should we take advice on sex from the Pope? If he knows anything about it, he shouldn't.

George Bernard Shaw

The average orgasm is only ten seconds long. The average frequency of intercourse is once or twice a week. That's twenty seconds a week, one-and-a-half minutes a month, eighteen minutes a year. In fifty years, that's about fifteen hours. For fifteen hours of ecstasy, we devote how many thousands of hours

to thinking about sex, worrying about sex, day-
dreaming about sex, planning for sex?

Alan Bauer

One orgasm in the bush is worth two in the hand.

Anonymous

I urge you to come faster than the wind
to mount my breast
and firmly dig and plough my body,
and don't let go until you've flushed me thrice.

Ancient Arab poem

Sex is nature's way of saying hello.

Anonymous

I wear two condoms all the time. Then when I'm
going to have sex, I take one off and I feel like a
wild man.

Dennis Miller

Love is the self-delusion we manufacture to justify
all the trouble we take to have sex.

Dan Greenburg

I begin every day thinking that I won't get laid.
Then if I do it's a pleasant surprise. If I don't, I
have the satisfaction of being right.

Greg Stone

No sex is better than bad sex.

Germaine Greer

Sex is like pizza. Even when it's lousy, it's still pretty
good.

Anonymous

The only way to feed on beauty is to feast one's
eyes upon it; and to man, beauty is a real and
essential food. It is a food which is assimilated into
his body and essential to his life, without which he
cannot live and be himself.

John S. Bayne

To me, the most exciting part of sex is getting the
bra off. After that it's just work.

"It's Like, You Know" TV show

She banged her fist on the wall and screamed,
"Oh, my God! I'm going to come! I started licking
her harder, and then all of a sudden she roared
like some kind of desperate mountain lion and her
pussy exploded. Water shot out everywhere. She
was coming like a spilled tanker, and it was the
coolest fucking thing I had ever seen in my life. I
just thought, "Oh my God, I love this girl. This is
the one! Every day after rehearsal, I would pick her
up in my van, we'd park somewhere quiet and she
would squirt everywhere. ...Eventually, my van
started to stink. I drove my mom to the store one
afternoon, and she kept asking what the smell was.
I had to pretend like I didn't know.

Tommy Lee

Why did God give us genitals if he wanted us to
think clearly?

Graham Greene

Sex is two plus two making five, rather than four.
Sex is the X ingredient that you can't define . . .

Marty Feldman

I find that the three major administrative problems
on a campus are sex for the students, athletics for
the alumni and parking for the faculty.
Clark Kerr,
President of the University of California, 1958

Beaches, beer and bikinis . . . sand, surf and sex.
Dave Mazur, on spring break in Ft. Lauderdale

How you settled your head athwart my hips,
And gently turn'd over upon me,
And parted the shirt from my bosom-bone,
And plunged your tongue to my bare-stript heart.
Walt Whitman

Reading is like the sex act – done privately and
often in bed.
Daniel J. Boorstin, Librarian of Congress

He was a sex junkie with an insatiable habit.
Gay Talese, talking about Hugh Hefner

Do what you love, the money will follow.
Marsha Sinetar

Yes, this was love, the ridiculous bouncing of the
buttocks and the wilting of the poor, insignificant
moist little penis.
D. H. Lawrence

If you want to lick the old woman's pot, you've got
to scratch her back.
Jamaican proverb

When my bed is empty
Makes me feel awful mean and blue
My springs are getting rusty
Living single like I do.

Bessie Smith, song lyric

tip top said he
don't stop said she
oh no said he
go slow said she

E. E. Cummings

Anyone who calls it "sexual intercourse" can't possibly
be interested in doing it. You might as well announce
you're ready for lunch by proclaiming, I'd like to do
some masticating and enzyme secreting."

Allan Sherman

It is all made of fantasy,
All made of passion, and all made of wishes.

William Shakespeare

. . . to talk about adults without talking about their
sex drives is like talking about a window without
glass.

Grace Metalious

Isn't talking about sex a little like dancing about
architecture?

John-Paul Sousa

Sex is a short cut to everything.

Anne Cummings

When both are locked in the embrace of love,
There is no separateness, no good or bad;
All thoughts vanish
With the onslaught of pure passion.

Kuttani Mahatmyan

Abstinence sows sand all over
The ruddy limbs and flaming hair;
But desire gratified
Plants fruits of life and beauty there.

William Blake

Without shame the man I like knows and avows the
    deliciousness of his sex,
Without shame the woman I like knows and avows hers.

Walt Whitman

Sexual desire is like a running stream, and the
stream of man and woman join and flow together
spontaneously. Desire is a pure thing like sunshine
or fire or rain.

Trailok Chandra Majupuria

I'm bare-boned and crazy for you . . .
Hike up your skirt a little more
And show your world to me
In a boy's dream . . .

Dave Matthews, song lyric

Tell him I've been too fucking busy – or vice versa.

Dorothy Parker, responding to an editor
who wanted her to write a story
while on her honeymoon

(Vote for) someone who has sex in only one
position – and doesn't enjoy it.

Maureen McCormick, in the role of
a mayoral candidate on "Son of the Beach"

No government has the right to tell its citizens
when or whom to love. The only queer people are
those who don't love anybody.

Rita Mae Brown

It is simpler to treat sex morally than reasonably.

Phyllis McGinley

Sex is not a moral question. For answers you don't
turn to a body of absolutes. The criterion should
not be, "Is it morally right or wrong?" but "Is it
socially feasible, is it personally healthy and
rewarding, will it enrich life?"

Grancolle Fisher

Before making love, in order to stimulate desire,
the woman should behave just as the man.
Whatever the man practices on the woman should
also be practiced on him by her.

The Kama Sutra

We need to get rid of the script that plagues even
the most sexually adventurous and evolved hetero-
sexuals: sex is all about vaginal intercourse. It's
leading up to that. It's going there. ...All body
parts, all sexual acts, all desires, all fantasies, all
erogenous zones...they're all on the table.

Tristan Taormino

Midnight, and love, and youth, and Italy!

Edward Bulwer-Lytton

Caressing above and patting below, kissing to the east and nibbling to the west, a thousand charms are revealed and a hundred cares forgotten.

Chinese Sexual Yoga

Sex will always be better, having been raised Catholic, because it will always be dirty.

John Waters

Sex isn't the answer! Sex is the question. "Yes" is the answer.

Anonymous

You know, love might make the world go round, folks, but sex certainly greases the poles.

Dennis Miller

I caused my husband's heart attack. In the middle of love-making I took the paper bag off my head. He dropped the Polaroid and keeled over and so did the hooker. It would have taken me half-an-hour to untie myself and call the paramedics, but fortunately the Great Dane could dial.

Joan Rivers

Do you know what a rodeo fuck is? A rodeo fuck is when you're fucking your wife you say to her, "I fucked your sister." And if you can stay on for one more minute – that's a rodeo fuck.

Rodney Dangerfield

In Europe intercourse between men and women is the result of love. In Oceania love is the result of intercourse. Which is right?

Paul Gauguin

Your daughter and the Moor are now making the beast with two backs.

William Shakespeare

꞊8꞊

Kinky Sex Involves The Use Of Duck Feathers, Perverted Sex Involves The Whole Duck

When I was growing up we had a petting zoo, and then we had a heavy-petting zoo for people who really liked the animals a lot.

Ellen DeGeneres

I'd rather do it with an animal than with a woman.

Bodil, star of Danish bestiality films

The very disgust of it turned me on.

Linda Lovelace, on bestiality

Promptly, Lotus Blossom insert its (the toy trumpet's) mouthpiece into her vagina and, for

her first number, blew a few notes on it, loud and
clear! . . . Going on with the show she inserted
about an inch of a banana into her vagina. She
then literally bit – yes, bit! – off piece after piece.
She now took three cigarettes from a pack,
inserted all three of them together in her vagina
and lit them with a match. Taking deep puffs, she
– believe it or not! – blew one perfectly formed
smoke ring after the other out of her pussy . . . She
took the tip of the bottle (of cola) into her vagina
as if it were a mouth and drank – yes, drank! –
about half the bottle. Then . . . she squirted the
cola in three or four jets clear across the room. As
if that was not yet enough, she piled up a bunch of
quarter-sized coins . . . lowered herself onto them
and made them disappear inside her . . . Then,
walking around the room, she released them one
by one, letting them drop clattering on the floor.

Phyllis and Eberhard Kronhausen,
describing Lotus Blossom,
the Pussy Acrobat of Taipei,
in "The Sex People"

(Sarah Bernhardt) demanded that her intimate
friends should keep her company in the narrow
box (a satin-lined rosewood coffin). Some of them
hesitated because this funereal furniture killed
their desires.

Marie Colombier

It is very disturbing indeed when you can't think of
any new perversions that you would like to practice.

James Dickey

Oh, I watch you there
Through the window
And I stare at you
You wear nothing
But you wear it so well
Tied up and twisted,
The way I'd like to be

Dave Matthews, song lyric

(She'd been expelled from the Marine Corps for) trying to fuck a platoon. Some captain or someone caught her after she'd done 90 men.

Bill Majors, talking about porn star Viper

Ouch! That felt good.

Karen E. Gordon

There is hardly anyone whose sexual life, if it were broadcast, would not fill the world at large with surprise and horror.

Somerset Maugham

You get a better class of person at orgies, because people have to keep in trim more. There is an awful lot of going round holding in your stomach, you know. Everybody is very polite to each other. The conversation isn't very good but you can't have everything.

Gore Vidal

There's nothing wrong with going to bed with somebody of your own sex. People should be very free with sex – they should draw the line at goats.

Elton John

It is perfect nonsense to say that sex should only be
carried on in the way animals do theirs (for
reproduction purposes).

Alan Watts

The only other creatures, beside humans, that
engage in recreational sex are dolphins and
chimpanzees. And why not? They're great
fucks. . . . Or so I've heard.

Dennis Miller

I've tried everything but coprophagia and
necrophilia, and I like kissing best.

John Waters

We are recorders and reporters of the facts – not
judges of the behavior we describe.

Alfred Kinsey, sex researcher

Someone asked me if I know what good clean fun
is. No, I don't know what good it is.

Judy Carne

I'm against group sex because I wouldn't know
where to put my elbows.

Martin Cruz Smith

If God had meant us to have group sex, he'd have
given us more organs.

Malcolm Bradbury

Great Babylon was naked
Ah! she stood there trembling for me
And Bethlehem inflamed us both

Like the shy one at some orgy
> *Leonard Cohen, song lyric*

At twenty-nine, Rodrigo Borgia (later to become
Pope Alexander VI) was rebuked by Pope Pius II
for appearing at an orgy in his cardinal's robes . . .
For 24,000 gold pieces Rodrigo sold a nobleman
permission to commit incest with his sister . . . At
the Vatican fifty whores danced nude and Rodrigo
(then Pope) gave prizes to the men who copulated
the most times with the prostitutes.
> *Burchard, Bishop of Ostia*

Nuns are sexy.
> *Madonna*

Forgive me now, Father
I just fucked a nun
Dressed her like an altar boy
And had me some fun
> *X-rated version of the lyrics to*
> *"The Wild Rover," an Irish folk song*

Our father is old, and there is no man on the earth
to come in to us as is the custom of all the earth.
Come, let us make our father drink wine, and we
will lie with him, that we may preserve the lineage
of our father.
> *The story of Lot as told in*
> *Genesis 19:31-32, The Bible*

Going to bed with Episcopalians is like ecclesiastical
necrophilia.
> *Reverend Walter Sundberg*

I'm too shy to express my sexual needs except over
the phone to people I don't know.

Garry Shandling

I tried phone sex and it gave me an ear infection.

Richard Lewis

It's been so long since I've made love I can't even
remember who gets tied up.

Joan Rivers

Some mornings it just doesn't seem worth chewing
through the leather straps.

Emo Philips

The variables are surprisingly few . . . One can
whip or be whipped; one can eat excrement or
quaff urine; mouth and private parts can be met in
this or that commerce. After that there is the grey
of morning and the sour knowledge that things
have remained fairly generally the same since man
first met goat and woman.

George Steiner

Sex is hardly ever just about sex.

Shirley MacLaine

Would you like to pet my pussy?

*Zsa Zsa Gabor, showing off her prized pussycat
on The Tonight Show*

Sure. Just move the damn cat off your lap.

Johnny Carson

Zeus performed acts with swans and heifers that would debar him from every London club except the Garrick or possibly the Naval and Military.

Stephen Fry

I believe that sex is a beautiful thing between two people. Between five, it's fantastic.

Woody Allen

He's such a hick he doesn't even have a trapeze in his bedroom.

Steve Martin

A partner evoked by sophisticated electric brain stimulation could be as real and much more satisfying than the boy or girl next door.

William Burroughs

I sometimes think that I should like
To be the seat on a girl's bike.

Anonymous

I'm all for bringing back the birch, but only between consenting adults.

Gore Vidal

Happiness consists of having many passions and many means of satisfying them.

Charles Fourier

I don't know if you've ever had a woman eat an apple while you were doing it. Well, you can imagine how that affects you.

Henry Miller

He doesn't even take his boots off, and sometimes we don't get into the bed. We stretch out on the floor. On the floor he is very erotic.

Eva Braun, talking about Adolph Hitler

"Beat me, beat me," begged the masochist.
"No," said the sadist.

Anonymous

Home is heaven and orgies are vile,
But you need an orgy, once in a while.

Ogden Nash

Between two evils, I always pick the one I never tried before.

Mae West

I'd have fucked anything, taken anything . . . I did. I'd take it, suck it, lick it, smoke it, shoot it, fall in love with it.

Janis Joplin

Never lie down with a woman who's got more troubles than you.

Nelson Algren

I have never been able to understand how a father could tenderly love his charming daughter without having slept with her at least once.

Casanova

One should try everything once, except incest and folk dancing.

Sir Arnold Bax

I would love to be whipped by you, Nora love!
James Joyce, from a love letter to his wife

Kinky sex involves the use of duck feathers.
Perverted sex involves the whole duck.
Lewis Grizzard

≈9≈

Never Trust A Man
With A Small Cock

Angry that his girlfriend had asked Truman Capote to autograph her breast, the boyfriend stormed up to the famous author, pulled out his dick and said, "Can you autograph this?"
"No," Capote replied, "but maybe I could initial it."

Science magazine came out with a report on the difference between men's and women's brains. Apparently, women are more controlled by a part of the brain called singletgyrus, and men are more controlled by a part of the brain known as the penis.

Jay Leno

Rub-a-dub-dub
Three men in a tub
And that's on a slow night
San Francisco bath house sign

Of that which man holds dear, nothing exceeds
the desires of the bedroom.
Chinese Sexual Yoga

Hung like a horse and could go all night.
Clara Bow, talking about Gary Cooper

Personally, given the choice between a donkey and
a chipmunk, I might choose the latter.
Sheilah Graham, to reassure her lover
(F. Scott Fitzgerald) that size isn't everything

In males, one of the most general causes of sexual
excitement is constipation . . . When this condition
is chronic, as in habitual constipation, the
unnatural excitement often leads to serious results.
Dr. J.H. Kellog, 1879

I want more in life than meeting a pretty face and
sitting down on it.
Harvey Fierstein

I don't believe most women are as quickly or as
indiscriminately aroused as most men are. It's a
peculiar male problem to want to copulate with
almost anything that moves.
Roy Scheider

If it moves then you fuck it.
Elvis Costello, song lyric

My schoolmates would make love to anything that moved, but I never saw any reason to limit myself.

Emo Philips

If I had a cock for a day, I'd get myself pregnant.

Germaine Greer

The Irish queer was cynically defined as a man who preferred women to drink. It might be redefined as a man who preferred women to talking.

David Hanley

If Clark (Gable) had one inch less, he'd be the queen of Hollywood instead of the king.

Carole Lombard

Women say it's not how much men have, but what we do with it. How many things can we do with it? What is it, a Cuisinart? It's got two speeds: forward and reverse.

Richard Jeni

One finger professionally, gentlemen; two fingers socially.

Ribald gynecologist's creed

Males cannot look at breasts and think at the same time.

Dave Barry

His schlang brings to mind the fire hoses along the corridors at school. Schlang: the word somehow captures the brutishness, the meatiness that I admire so, the sheer mindless, weighty and unselfconscious

dangle of that living piece of hose through which he
passes water as thick and strong as rope.

Philip Roth

Down, wanton, down! Have you no shame
That at the whisper of Love's name,
Or Beauty's, presto! up you raise
Your angry head and stand at gaze?

Robert Graves

Is that a gun in your pocket, or are you just glad to
see me?

Mae West

A man is two people, himself and his cock. A man
always takes his friend to the party. Of the two, the
friend is the nicer, being more able to show his
feelings.

Beryl Bainbridge

I wouldn't sue anyone for saying I had a big prick.
No man would. In fact I might pay them to do it.

Joe Orton

Stiff standing on the bed,
First it's white, and then it's red.
There's not a lady in the land
That would not take it in her hand.

Anonymous

There is nothing about which men lie so much
about as their sexual powers. In this at least every
man is, what in his heart he would like to be, a
Casanova.

Somerset Maugham

Only the male intellect, clouded by sexual impulse, could call the undersized, narrow-shouldered, broad-hipped, and short-legged sex the fair sex.

Arthur Schopenhauer

The big mistake men make is that when they turn thirteen or fourteen and all of a sudden they've reached puberty, they believe that they like women. Actually, you're just horny. It doesn't mean you like women any more at twenty-one than you did at ten.

Jules Feifer

And they (the men of Sodom) called to Lot and said to him, "Where are the men who came to you tonight? Bring them out to us that we may know them carnally."

So Lot went out to them . . . and said, "Please, my brethren, do not do so wickedly! See now, I have two daughters who have not known a man; please, let me bring them out to you, and you may do to them as you wish; only do nothing to these men, since this is the reason they have come under the shadow of my roof."

And they said, "Stand back!"

Genesis 19:5-9, The Bible

I'll take a guy who doesn't talk at all, please. Sold!

Lucy Liu

I don't say anything during sex. I've been told not to.

Chevy Chase

After he was deposed, the king's possessions, including a vast amount of pornography and the world's largest stamp collection, brought over one million dollars at auction. . . . He had attempted intercourse with over 5,000 women in his lifetime . . . He later married Narriman Sadek, a sixteen-year-old.

Hugh McLeave,
biographer of Farouk I of Egypt (1920-1965)

A man can be happy with any woman as long as he does not love her.

Oscar Wilde

'Tis strange what a man may do, and a woman yet think him an angel.

William Makepeace Thackeray

The phallus is the primary sensorial organ of the soul, it creates man, it gives birth to the imagination, it unleashes the thinking faculty in the individual.

Lotus de Peralta

I'm never through with a girl until I've had her three ways.

President John F. Kennedy

Give it to me harder! I can take it like a man!
Unidentified porno actress, during anal sex

Give a man a free hand and he'll run it all over you.
Mae West

Also his lovely young cock there so simply. I wouldn't mind taking him in my mouth if nobody was looking, as it was asking you to suck it, so clean

and white he looked . . . I would too, in half-a-
minute. Even if some of it went down. Well, it's
only like a gruel or the dew – there's no danger.
Besides he'd be so clean compared with those pigs
of men I suppose never dream of washing it from
one year's end to the other . . .

James Joyce

Most of my male friends are gay, and that seems
perfectly natural to me. I mean, who wouldn't like
a cock?

Valerie Perrine

The thrust of the buttocks, surely it was a little
ridiculous. If you were a woman, and apart in all
the business, surely that thrusting of the man's
buttocks was supremely ridiculous.

D.H. Lawrence

He was one of those men who come in a door and
make any woman with them look guilty.

F. Scott Fitzgerald

What is my favorite romantic spot? You mean in the
whole world or on somebody's body?

Jackie Mason

Love, for too many men of our time, consists of
sleeping with a seductive woman, one who is
properly endowed with the right distribution of
curves and conveniences . . .

Ashley Montagu

When you're not talking politics, what do you and
your father (President Bush) talk about?

David Fink, reporter for the Hartford Courant,
at the 1988 Republican Convention

Pussy.

George W. Bush

Imagine . . . hanging the stones of a man outside,
where they are forever getting themselves
knocked, pinched, and bruised. Any decent
mechanic would have put them in the exact
center of the body, protected by an envelope twice
as thick as even a Presbyterian's skull. Moreover,
consider certain parts of the female – always too
large or too small. The elemental notion of
standardization seems to have never presented
itself to the celestial Edison.

H. L. Mencken

If I don't do it every day, I get a headache.

Willie Nelson

Macho does not prove mucho.

Zsa Zsa Gabor

Intercourse is the pure, sterile, formal expression
of men's contempt for women.

Andrea Dworkin

A gentleman is a patient wolf.

Henrietta Tiarks

You can't tell your friend you've been cuckolded;
even if he doesn't laugh at you, he may put the
information to personal use.

Montaigne

Women think of being a man as a gift. It is a duty.
Even making love can be a duty. A man has always
got to get it up, and love isn't always enough.

Norman Mailer

Behold – the penis mightier than the sword.

Mark Twain

In good faith, he cares not what mischief he does,
if his weapon be out: he will foin like any devil; he
will spare neither man, woman nor child.

William Shakespeare

Like iron or some kind of a thick crowbar standing
all the time. He must have eaten oysters. I think a
few dozen . . . Oh, I never in all my life felt anyone
had one the size of that, it made you feel full up.
Whose idea making us like that with a big hole in
the middle of us? Like a stallion driving it up into
you. Because that's all they want out of you with
that determined viscous look in his eye . . . Still he
hasn't such a tremendous amount of spunk in him
when I made him pull it out and do it on me,
considering how big it is.

James Joyce

Men ought to be more conscious of their bodies as
an object of delight.

Germaine Greer

It would be less demanding, enslaving, perplexing
and strenuous for a healthy male to screw a
thousand women in his lifetime than to try to
please one, and the potential for failure would be
less.

Irma Kurtz

Men are creatures with two legs and eight hands.
Jayne Mansfield

I love the male body, it's better designed than the male mind.
Andrea Newman

It's well for a man, all the amount of pleasure they get from a woman's body. We're so round and white for them always. I wished I was one myself for a change. Just to try with that thing they have swelling upon you so hard – at the same time so soft when you touch it.
James Joyce

An erection at will is the moral equivalent of a valid credit card.
Dr. Alex Comfort

I used too much of that delay cream once and I'm still waiting for an orgasm from a drive-in movie handjob from August of '72.
Dennis Miller

Part of the loot went for women, part for gambling. The rest I spent foolishly.
George Raft

I don't like to admit it, but if a girl baited her trap with sex, she'd catch me every time – and it's unlikely this will ever cease to work.
Willie Nelson

She came to me and took me, tumbled me
beneath her and rubbed me with astonishing
passion, until all my soul rushed into a part of me
which you can divine, my Lord. I set to the work
required of me, the work under my hand; I
reduced that which there was to reduce, I broke
that which there was to break, and ravished that
which there was to ravish. . . . My rascal earned his
names of ram, smith, stunner, sweet calamity, long
one, iron, weeper, workman, horner, rubber, old
irresistible, staff, prodigious tool, pathfinder, blind
fighter, young sword, great swimmer, nightingale,
thick-neck father, father of nerves, him of the
large eggs, old man with a turban, bald head,
father of thrusts, father of delights, father of
terrors, cock of the silence, daddy's little one, the
poor man's wealth, old muscle of caprice, and
mighty sugar-stick.

A Thousand and One Arabian Nights

God grant me a prick so that I won't be lacking.

Medieval song lyric

A lot of time has been wasted on arguing over
which came first: the chicken or the egg. It was
undoubtedly the rooster.

Paul Dickson

Men are essentially dogs and women are essentially
cats. Men are more capable of sniffing a new
acquaintance's asshole on the sidewalk. Women are
sleeker.

Martin Mull

Car profiles gave me erections, sports statistics gave me erections, the topology of hillsides gave me erections, and so did . . . several species of birds and one or two trees. That's what it's like to be a young male.

Brian Fawcett

When the prick stands up, the brain goes to sleep.

Yiddish proverb

If a man drops his trousers he's arrested. If a woman drops her dress she's paid.

Dennis Prager

Wearing a condom is like shaking hands with gloves on.

Anonymous

A stiff prick has no conscience.

Anonymous

It's not the men in my life that counts, it's the life in my men.

Mae West

Many a man leaves the straight and narrow path to follow a woman who isn't built that way.

Anonymous

Never trust a doctor who tries to take your temperature with his finger.

David Letterman

Outside of every thin woman is a fat man trying to get in.

Katherine Whitehorn

German men . . . try to give you the impression
that to accompany them from the airplane and
share their bed would be a contribution toward
some better, super-world.

Trudy Baker and Rachel Jones

My brain? It's my second favorite organ.

Woody Allen

Do you have any African in you? Would you like
some?

Anonymous

The smallest things give me a great cockstand – a
whorish movement of your mouth, a little brown
stain on the seat of your white drawers . . . to feel
your hot lecherous lips sucking away at me, to fuck
between your two rosy-tipped bubbies . . .

James Joyce, from a love letter to his wife

Whatever is hidden should be made naked.

Dylan Thomas

How well a soft and libertine voice will erect your
member. It is as good as fingers . . .

Juvenal

Teenage boys, goaded by their surfing
hormones . . . run in packs. They have only a brief
season of exhilarating liberty between control by
their mothers and control by their wives.

Camille Paglia

Like all young men, you greatly exaggerate the difference between one young woman and another.

George Bernard Shaw

My God, no. I don't have the strength.

President John F. Kennedy,
when asked if he tried to seduce every woman he met

I was always interested in proportion. When I was 15, I took off my clothes and looked in the mirror. When I stared at myself naked, I realized that to be perfectly proportioned I would need twenty inch arms to match the . . . rest of me.

Arnold Schwarzenegger

She'll never know it's there. The condom that is.

Sheik condom ad

Male sexual response is far brisker and more automatic. It is triggered easily by things – like putting a quarter in a vending machine.

Dr. Alex Comfort

He (Jimi Hendrix) has got just about the biggest rig I've ever seen! . . . In fact, I believe the reason we couldn't get his rig out was that it wouldn't get soft!

Plaster Casters, two girls who made
plaster molds of the erections of rock stars

I said (to Peter O'Toole) afterwards that if Lawrence (of Arabia) had looked like him there would have been many more than twelve Turks lining up for the buggering scene.

Noel Coward

The problem was that when I was young I used to like to do it standing up and, if I had ever done it with him, he would have been jabbing me in the knees.

Josephine Baker,
recalling a short male admirer

When you're going to pull out on someone, tell them first.

John Irving

What's the definition of eternity? The time between when you cum and when she leaves.

Bryant Gumbel

Condoms should be sized like olives: large, extra large, and colossal.

Anonymous

A hard man is good to find.

Mae West

To blurt it out in a word – we want laying.

Aristophanes

A man with an erection is in no need of advice.

Italian proverb

I've had my cock sucked by five of the big (male) names in Hollywood.

James Dean

I don't understand it at all. I'm a cunt man myself.

Duke Ellington

I wouldn't want a penis. It would be like having a third leg.

Madonna

Hemingway's big problem all his life was he was worried about his penis. The size of it.
Sidney Franklin, holding up his pinky finger

The sexual organ therefore has a double role: the inferior one of procreation, and the superior one of contacting the divine state by means of the ecstasy caused by pleasure.

Alain Daniélou

I want a man who's kind and understanding. Is that too much to ask of a millionaire?

Zsa Zsa Gabor

She sleeps with others because she loves them, but for money, only with me!

Ferenc Molnar

There are two things no man will admit he can't do well: drive and make love.

Stirling Moss

What two words will immediately empty a men's rest room? Nice dick.

Anonymous

There's a new book out called *1,001 Sex Secrets Men Should Know.* I think most women would actually settle for three: slow down, turn off the TV, call out the right name.

Jay Leno

The male sex, as a sex, does not universally appeal
to me.

Katherine Hepburn

I never trust a man unless I've got his pecker in my
pocket.

President Lyndon B. Johnson

A man is by nature a sexual animal. I've always had
my share of pets.

Mae West

To call a man an animal is to flatter him; he's a
machine, a walking dildo.

Valerie Solanas

You should never turn down a glorious erection
like this! You should applaud it!

Fernando Lamas

Whew! What a bony butt.

Michael Douglas,
commenting on his nude scene

There is no sin in loving men. Only pain.

Calista Flockhart, on "Ally McBeal"

I have a man I never could trust. He cheats so much
I'm not even sure this baby I'm carrying is his.

Letter to Dear Abby

Women need a reason to have sex. Men just need
a place.

Billy Crystal

He was a man and he was horny. But I repeat myself.
Conversation overheard at a women's college

The difference between a man and a turd is that after you've laid a turd you don't have to hug it.
Julian Barnes

Arousal is a miracle . . . don't try to hide it. (It's) an unsolicited endorsement, a standing ovation, a spontaneous demonstration.
Playboy

Our great flaw is our inability to commit. We see a woman: "Yes, I will love you and devote my life to you forever and . . . wait . . . there goes another one!"
Brad Stine

Man is the only animal that blushes. Or needs to.
Mark Twain

Even dirty old men need love.
Graffito

Every man needs two women: a quiet homemaker and a thrilling nymph.
Iris Murdoch

There's nothing better than dropping a load in somebody you like, you know?
Andrew Dice Clay

Even a rat likes to go into a different hole once in a while.
Anonymous

There are two things a real man likes – danger and play; and he likes woman because she is the most dangerous of playthings.

Friedrich Nietzsche

Italian men have to make sure you know they've got a penis.

W. H. Auden

Let's forget about the six feet and talk about the seven inches.

Mae West

Never trust a man with a small cock.

Jean Cocteau

ᵇ10ᵇ

Women Are Made To Be Loved, Not Understood

Despite my thirty years of research into the feminine soul, I have not yet been able to answer the great question that has never been answered: what does a woman want?

Sigmund Freud

What do women want? Shoes.

Mimi Pond

I would say that the majority of women (happily for society) are not much troubled with sexual feeling of any kind.

Dr. William Acton, 1857

Madam, you have between your legs an instrument
capable of giving pleasure to thousands – and all
you can do is scratch it.

Sir Thomas Beecham

I rely on my personality for birth control.

Liz Winston

All women think they're ugly, even pretty women.
A man who understood this could fuck more
women than Don Giovanni. They *all* think their
cunts are ugly . . . They all find fault with their
figures . . . Even models and actresses, even women
you think are so beautiful that they have nothing to
worry about do worry all the time.

Erica Jong

My soul is bound
By the scents of her body,
Jasmine and musk
And rose of her body,
Amber and nard,
The scents of her body.

A Thousand and One Arabian Nights

Were kisses all the joys in bed,
One woman would another wed.

William Shakespeare

Two men – yes – I can see they've got something to
take hold of. But two women – that's impossible.
You can't have two insides having an affair!

Lydia Lopokova

Because her need to love and to be loved is smoldering and constant as a vestal fire, the young female is more randy than the male, whose lust rises and falls according to what is on offer.

Irma Kurtz

As for me, I dreamed simply of a dark-haired man bending over me to brush my lips with his burning red mouth and I woke up overwhelmed, palpitating and happier than I had ever imagined I could possibly be.

George Sand

How fair and how pleasant you are.
O love, with your delights!
This stature of yours is like a palm tree,
And your breasts like its clusters.
I said, "I will go up to the palm tree,
I will take hold of its branches."

Song of Solomon 7:6-8, The Bible

With women, I've got a long bamboo pole with a leather loop on the end of it. I slip the loop around their necks so they can't get away or come too close. Like catching snakes.

Marlon Brando

Woman, observing that her mate went out of his way to make himself entertaining, rightly surmised that sex had something to do with it. From that she logically concluded that sex was recreational. (The small hardy band of girls who failed to get this point were responsible for the popularity of women's field hockey.)

James Thurber and E.B. White

Underneath it all you longed to be annihilated by
love, to be swept off your feet, to be filled up by a
giant prick spouting sperm, soapsuds, silks and
satins, and, of course, money.

Erica Jong

It is a truth universally acknowledged among
women that any man in possession of a good
fortune must be in want of a wife.

Jane Austen

I remember the first time I told you that I named
my vagina Mona, because it sounded like sorrow,
like the word melancholy . . .

Elise D'Haene

Clits up!

Susie Bright

In real life, women are always trying to mix
something up with sex – religion, babies, or hard
cash; it is only men who long for sex separated out,
without rings or strings.

Katherine Whitehorn

Men are brought up to command, women to
seduce.

Sally Kempton

A woman is a ship with two holes in her bottom.

Olive Schreiner

You have the eyes of Hera,
the hands of Athena,

the breasts of Aphrodite.
Blessed is the man who looks upon you.
Thrice blessed is the man who hears you talk.
A demi-god is the man who kisses you.
A god the man who takes you into bed.

Rutinos

I kiss every woman four times. Once for each
cheek.

Duke Ellington

When a man puts his penis into a woman's vagina it
is as if he put his finger into her brain, stirred it
'round and 'round. Her whole nature is affected.

Olive Schreiner

. . . the kind of womb I want to marry.
Napoleon Boneparte, about his second wife,
the eighteen-year-old Marie Louise of Austria

It is amazing how complete is the delusion that
beauty is goodness.

Leo Tolstoy

Obee,
in your vast fields
are the lilies as sweet
as the mouth of this girl?
Saint Manikkavacakar of Tamil

She was charming, but she spoke only English.
Accustomed to loving only with all my senses, I
could not indulge in love without including my
sense of hearing.

Casanova

Third, if her vital essence wishes to be stirred up through love-making, she will begin to move her body up and down rhythmically. Fourth, if her heart's desire is to be completely satisfied, then profuse moisture will be emitted from her Jade Gate, sufficient even to wet her clothes. Fifth, if she is ready to reach orgasm, she will stretch her body like an animal, and close her eyes.

Secret Methods of the Plain Girl,
an Ancient Chinese text

The Vaginas Are Coming.

Heather Santmire, title of newspaper story

To enter life by way of the vagina is as good a way as any.

Henry Miller

When a woman becomes a scholar, there is usually something wrong with her sex organs.

Friedrich Nietzsche

A little still she strove, and much repented,
And whispering, "I will ne'er consent" –
consented.

Lord Byron

She is descended from a long line that her mother listened to.

Gypsy Rose Lee

I am happy now that Charles calls on my bedchamber less frequently than of old. As it is, I now endure but two calls a week and when I hear

his steps outside my door I lie down on my bed,
close my eyes, open my legs and think of England.

Alice, Lady Hillingdon

Ladies don't move.

English proverb

After the big eruption comes the afterglow. This is
the time women want to hear sweet nothings like,
"Run away with me forever, cara mia! Instead, we
hear stuff like, "Boy, did I ever lose a big load!" "I
totally blew my nuts" or "That was so much better
than my hand!"

Anka Radakovich

And I'm your barefoot wench for a whole week...
Now you grab me by the ankles.
Now you work your way up the legs
And come to pierce me at my hunger mark.

Anne Sexton, from the poem "Barefoot"

That's a fair thought to lie between maids' legs.

William Shakespeare

The river of life flows through the meadows of Eden,
And the meadows of Eden are below her garment,
The moon is beneath her mantle.
Her body is a song of colors:
Carnation of roses answers to silver,
Black ripe berries
And new-cut sandalwood
Are one note.

The man who takes her is more blessed
Than the God who gave her;

And He is continually called Blessed.
A Thousand and One Arabian Nights

I kissed my first girl and smoked my first cigarette on the same day. I haven't had time for tobacco since.
Arturo Toscanini

She embraces him with such force that their bodies become a single body.
The Kama Sutra

Ah, everything was blessed and beautified by her presence.
Friedrich Holderlin

A woman talks to one man, looks at a second, and thinks of a third.
Bhartrihari

A couple of women moved in across the hall from me. One is a middle-aged gym teacher and the other is a social worker in her mid-twenties. These two women go everywhere together and I've never seen a man go into their apartment or come out. Do you think they could be Lebanese?
Letter to Dear Abby

How beautiful are your feet in sandals,
O prince's daughter!
The curves of your thighs are like jewels,
The work of the hands of a skillful workman.
Your naval is a rounded goblet . . .
Your two breasts are like two fawns,
Twins of a gazelle.
Song of Solomon 7:1-3, The Bible

My mother didn't breast-feed me. She said she
liked me as a friend.

Rodney Dangerfield

No woman needs intercourse; few escape it.

Andrea Dworkin

Fair, agreeable, good friend,
When will I have you in my power,
Lie beside you for an evening,
And kiss you amorously?
Be sure I'd feel a strong desire
To have you in my husband's place
Provided you had promised me
To do everything I wished.

La Comtessa de Dia

Being a woman is of special interest to aspiring
male transsexuals. To actual women, it's simply a
good excuse not to play football.

Fran Lebowitz

All jobs should be open to everybody, unless they
actually require a penis or vagina.

Florynce Kennedy

I'd like to have a girl, and I'm saving my money so I
can get a good one.

Bob Nickman

My DKNY black skirt is pushed up around my waist,
my DKNY black tights scrunched at my ankles, an
electric toothbrush dangling like a sorry limp cock
between my legs . . .

Elise D'Haene

One night in the darkness, I demanded my heart
again from thy tresses. I beheld thy cheek, and
drank the cup of thy mouth. I drew quickly to my
breast, and thy tresses blazed in flame; I pressed lip
to lip, and gave for thy ransom my soul and heart.

Haféz

I do not believe the beauty of another lady can
equal hers, because the rose, when it blooms, is no
fresher than she; her body is well made and of
gracious proportions, and her eyes and her mouth
are the light of the world.

Raimon de Miraval

The most important quality is that she doesn't
know she's beautiful, of if she does, she doesn't
believe it. There's nothing more unattractive – for
me – and less sexual than a woman who knows
she's a beauty, who knows men are looking at her.

Roger Vadim

There's a new book out called *The Art of the Female
Orgasm*. The problem with it is men can't seem to
finish it and women think it should be read repeatedly.

Jay Leno

Sex pleasure in women...is a kind of magic spell; it
demands complete abandon; if words or move-
ments oppose the magic of caresses, the spell is
broken.

Simone de Beauvoir

I've looked at a lot of women with lust. I've
committed adultery in my heart many times.
President Jimmy Carter

He that but looketh on a plate of ham and eggs to
lust after it, hath already committed breakfast with
it in his heart.
C. S. Lewis

Oh, you man of all man,
Who fillest me with pleasure.
Oh, you soul of my soul, go on with fresh vigor,
For you must not yet withdraw it from me;
Leave it there,
And this day will then be free of all sorrow.
The Perfumed Garden

The best thing a cunt can be is small and
unobtrusive: The anxiety about the bigness of the
penis is only equaled by anxiety about the smallness
of the cunt. No woman wants to find out that she
has a twat like a horse-collar.
Germaine Greer

She would serve after a long voyage at sea.
William Shakespeare

Busts and bosoms I have known
Of various shapes and sizes,
From grievous disappointments
To jubilant surprises.
Anonymous

Men reach their sexual peak at 18. Women reach
theirs at 35. Do you get the feeling that God is
playing a practical joke?

Rita Rudner

Though a woman is naturally reserved and keeps
her feelings concealed, yet when she gets on top of
a man she should show all her love and desire.

The Kama Sutra

For women, eating has taken on the sinful status
once reserved for sex.

Anonymous

Their two hearts beat as one,
They pressed together fragrant shoulders
And touched each other's cheeks.
He grasped that perfumed breast,
Smooth as the softest down,
And found it perfect.

Chin P'ing Mei

There are two kinds of women: those who want
power in the world, and those who want power in
bed.

Jacqueline Kennedy Onassis

How delicious is woman, when artfully played
upon; how capable is she of producing the most
exquisite harmonies, of executing the most
complicated variations of love, and giving the most
divine of erotic pleasures.

Ananga Ranga

I wanted to be the first woman to burn her bra, but
it would have taken the fire department four days
to put it out.

Dolly Parton

When she raises her eyebrows it's as if she's taking
off all her clothes.

Colette

When he sees me in heat he quickly comes to me,
Then he opens my thighs and kisses my belly,
And puts his tool in my hand to make it knock at
  my door.
Soon he is in the cave, and I feel pleasure
  approaching.
He shakes me and thrills me, and hotly we both
  are working,
And he says, "Receive my seed!" and I answer, "Oh,
  give it, beloved one!"

Sheikh Nefzawi, early 16ᵗʰ Century

I think women see me on the cover of magazines
and think I never have a pimple or bags under my
eyes. You have to realize that's after two hours of
hair and makeup, plus retouching. Even I don't
wake up looking like Cindy Crawford.

Cindy Crawford

That's not me you're in love with. That's my image.
You don't even know me.

Kelly McGillis

Nowadays, when models open up and display their
sex, they still look straight into the sucker's eyes,

just the way a grocer does when he assures his
customer the mango is ripe.

Irma Kurtz

What do women find most attractive in a man? A
big, throbbing wallet.

John-Paul Sousa

To read the papers and magazines, you would
think we were almost worshipping the female
bosom.

Reverend Billy Graham

Don't count your boobies until they are hatched.

James Thurber

We are becoming the men we wanted to marry.

Gloria Steinem

Feminism encourages women to leave their
husbands, kill their children, practice witchcraft,
destroy capitalism and become lesbians.

Pat Robertson

I have a big flaw in that I am attracted to thin, tall,
good-looking men who have one common
denominator. They must be lurking bastards.

Edna O'Brien

There is nothing so sweet in the world
As a woman's cunt, you can be sure of it.
She carries the large urn
That is worth all of a castle's gold.

Gautier Le Lou

No woman is worth more than a fiver unless
you're in love with her. Then she's worth all she
costs you.

Somerset Maugham

I never expected to see the day when girls would
get sunburned in the places they do today.

Will Rogers

Women should be obscene and not heard.

John Lennon

Women now have the right to plant rolled-up
dollar bills in the jockstraps of steroid-sodden male
strippers.

Howard Ogden

Thus woman's secrets I've surveyed
And let them see how curiously they're made,
And that, tho' they of different sexes be,
Yet on the whole they are the same as we.
For those that have the strictest searchers been,
Find women are but men turned outside in;
And men, if they but cast their eyes about,
May find they're women with their inside out.

Aristotle

The degree of attention which breasts receive . . .
makes women unduly anxious about them. They
can never be just right; they must always be too
small, too big, the wrong shape, too flabby. The
characteristics . . . must be faked somehow or
another. Reality is either gross or scrawny.

Germaine Greer

In itself (the vagina) had an erotic appearance,
like the inside of a giraffe's ear or a tropical fruit
not much prized by the locals.

Kingsley Amis

The vagina is made so artificial that it can
accommodate itself to any penis, so that it will give
way to a long one, meet a short one, widen to a
thick one, constringe to a small one: so that every
man might well enough lie with any woman, and
every woman with any man.

The Anatomy of Human Bodies Epitomised, 1682

There is no sign that her acting would ever have
progressed beyond the scope of the restless
shoulders and the protuberant breasts; her body
technique was the gangster's technique – she toted
a breast like a man totes a gun.

Graham Greene, writing about Jean Harlow

Her body was a weapon, not a fatal weapon. More
like a stun gun.

Madonna

He twisted my nipples as though tuning a radio.

Lisa Alther

Take off your cloak and your hat
And your shoes, and draw up at my hearth
Where never woman sat.

I have made the fire up bright;
Let us leave the rest in the dark
And sit by firelight.

The wine is warm in the hearth;
The flickers come and go.
I will warm your limbs with kisses
Until they glow.

D. H. Lawrence

A man needs the sexual conquest to prove that he
can still do it, that he can still get it up . . . We
don't have to prove it. And very often we'll sleep
with someone, not so much because we're turned
on, but because we really want companionship, or
we want the feeling of someone in bed with us.

Princess Elizabeth of Yugoslavia

I believe it was Galen who said that all animals are
sad after coitus except for the female human and
the rooster.

William Redfield

It's a sort of bloom on a woman. If you have it, you
don't need to have anything else; and if you don't
have it, it doesn't much matter what else you have.

James M. Barrie

Venus plays tricks on lovers with her game of
images which never satisfy.

Lucretius

Full frontal nudity . . . has now become accepted
by every branch of the theatrical profession with
the possible exception of lady accordion players.

Dennis Norden

All giggle, blush, half pertness, and half pout.

Lord Byron

You don't satisfy a girl with presents and flirting,
unless knees bang against knees and his locks into
hers with a flushing thrust.

Ancient Arab poem

It is like a purple flower of crimson, full of honey
and perfume. It is like a hydra of the sea, living
and soft, open at night. It is the humid grotto, the
shelter always warm, the asylum where man rests
on his march toward death.

Peter Louys

THE CREATION OF PUSSY
Seven wise men with knowledge so fine
Created a pussy to their design.
First was a butcher, smart with a wit.
Using a knife, he gave it a slit.
Second was a: carpenter, strong and bold.
With a hammer and chisel he gave it a hole.
Third was a tailor, tall and thin.
Using red velvet, he lined it within.
Fourth was a hunter, short and stout.
With a piece of fox fur he lined it without.
Fifth was a fisherman, nasty as hell.
Threw in a fish and gave it a smell.
Sixth was a preacher whose name was McGee.
Touched it and blessed it and said it could pee.
Last came a sailor, a dirty little runt.
He sucked it and fucked it and called it a cunt.

Unattributed limerick

There's really no reason to have a woman on a tour
unless they've got a job to do. The only other
reason is to screw. Otherwise they get bored, they
just sit around and moan.

Mick Jagger

If you make a proposal which in England would
bring a box on the ear from the meekest of virgins
to a Spanish girl, she thanks you for the honour
you intend her, and replies, "Wait till I am married,
and I shall be too happy."

Lord Byron

Women sometimes forgive those who force an
opportunity, never those who miss it.

Count Charles Talleyrand

No woman is so naked as one you can see to be
naked underneath her clothes.

Michael Frayn

What's getting maximally stimulated? The tip of
the penis moving in and out. Meanwhile the
clitoris is going, "Hello! What about me?"

Lana Holstein, MD

There are many women who have never had an
intrigue, but there are scarcely any who have had
no more than one.

La Rochefoucauld

Sex is first of all a very visual thing. A man walks
through the door, and I think, yes I would, no I
wouldn't. And any woman who says she doesn't
think that way, at least for a second, is a liar.

Soraya Khashoggi

The only place men want depth in women is in her décolletage.

Zsa Zsa Gabor

Man regards woman with intellectual contempt and sexual passion, both equally merited. Woman welcomes the passion but resents the contempt. She wishes to be rid of the discredit attached to her little brain, while retaining the credit attached to her large bosom.

A. E. Houseman

Feminine passion is to masculine as an epic is to an epigram.

Karl Kraus

Women speak easily of platonic love; but, while they appear to esteem it highly, there is not a single ribbon of their toilette that does not drive platonism from our hearts.

Auguste Ricard

Chemical analysis of women: Seldom found in natural state. Surface coated with paint and other chemical compounds. Low freezing point, but also highly explosive. Extremely active when in the vicinity of opposite sex. Probably the most powerful seducing agent known. Illegal to own more than one specimen.

Anonymous

Since maids, in modesty, say "No" to that
Which they would have the profferer construe
"Aye."

William Shakespeare

I have heard the wish expressed that one could be a girl, and a good-looking girl, between the ages of thirteen and twenty-two, and after that become a man.

Jean De La Bruyere

The basic Female Body comes with the following accessories: garter belt, panti-girdle, crinoline, camisole, bustle, brassiere, stomacher, chemise, virgin zone, spike heels, nose ring, veil, kid gloves, fishnet stockings, fichu, bandeau, Merry Widow, weepers, chokers, barrettes, bangles, beads, lorgnette, feather boa, basic black, compact, Lycra stretch one-piece modesty panel, designer peignoir, flannel nightie, lace teddy, bed, head.

Margaret Atwood

Anyone who says he can see through women is missing a lot.

Groucho Marx

Honestly, I walk around my house naked, so I'm not very modest or whatever. I think the body's a beautiful thing, and you should not hide yourself. . . . You should be proud of your sexuality.

Britney Spears

The great discovery of the age is that women like it too.

Hugh MacDiarmid

In her is the lyre,
In her is the rose,
In her is the harmonious science,

In her we breathe
The vital perfume of all things.

Rubén Dario

As Abe Martin says, women is just like elephants; I
like to look at 'em, but I'd sure hate to own one.

Will Rogers

Why own a cow when you can buy the milk?

Anonymous

Little girl: "Mommy, mommy! I don't have what
Billy has." To which her mother responded, "Don't
worry. As long as you've got what you have, you can
get as many as you want of what Billy has."

Anonymous

A mechanic comes up to me with a dipstick. I ask
him what he's going to do. He says, "I have to put
this in your thing." I said not without dinner and a
movie first.

Suzy Sorra

Many years ago I chased a woman for almost two
years, only to discover her tastes were exactly like
mine: We were both crazy about girls.

Groucho Marx

You wanna know the secret of life? The saliva of
young girls.

Tony Curtis

Just because I'm young doesn't mean I can't be
sexy.

Britney Spears

My Heart Belongs To Daddy

Cole Porter, song title

I hate a woman who offers herself because she
ought to do so, and cold and dry, thinks of her
sewing when she's making love.

Ovid

We still have these double standards where the
emphasis is all on the male's sexual appetites – that
it's OK for him to collect as many scalps as he can
before he settles down and "pays the price." If a
woman displays the same attitude, all the epithets
that exist in the English language are laid at her
door, and with extraordinary bitterness.

Glenda Jackson

. . . there's really no positive English word for
female sexuality.

Brittany Andrews

Miss Goddard was the mistress of a school . . .
where young ladies for enormous pay might be
screwed out of health and into vanity.

Jane Austen

Amazing! Astonishing! Still can't get over the
fantastic idea that when you are looking at a girl,
you are looking at somebody who is guaranteed to
have on her – a cunt! They all have cunts! Right
under their dresses! Cunts – for fucking.

Philip Roth

Starlet is the name for any woman under thirty not actively employed in a brothel.

Ben Hecht

A woman gets her hair done, puts on makeup, tummy toner, a short skirt and high heels, then says she wants to find a man who loves me for me.

Robert G. Lee

She that paints her face, thinks of her tail.

Benjamin Franklin

My God! We do smell like fish.

One lesbian to another

Spring has come and the flowers are brilliant with color,
Responding to the rhythms of love, your supple
  body moves.
Opening, opening is that most precious bud;
My drops of dew help your peony bloom.

Chang Sheng

I will have nought to do whether with lover or husband . . . albeit he come to me with an erection . . . I will live at home unbulled.

*Aristophanes,
reporting a vow taken by women
to withhold sex in order to stop war*

A woman can become a man's friend only in the following stages – first an acquaintance, next a mistress, and only then a friend.

Anton Chekhov

The fickleness of the women I love is only equaled by
the infernal constancy of the women who love me.

>   *George Bernard Shaw*

"Yes," I answered you last night;
"No," this morning, sir, I say:
Colors seen by candlelight
Will not look the same by day.

>   *Elizabeth Barrett Browning*

I heard a man say that brigands demand your
money or your life, whereas women require both.

>   *Samuel Butler*

Remember, you're fighting for this woman's honor,
which is probably more than she ever did.

>   *Groucho Marx*

Many a woman will fight for her honor until the
man is just about ready to give up.

>   *Anonymous*

Thank heaven for little girls!
For little girls get bigger every day.

>   *Alan Jay Lerner*

There's a difference between beauty and charm: a
beautiful woman is one I notice, a charming
woman is one who notices me.

>   *John Erskine*

A flirt always notices a man in such a way that he
notices her.

>   *Anonymous*

Suddenly he lunged and reached the innermost
Citadel, for within the Gate of Womanhood there
is a Citadel, like the heart of a flower, which if
touched by the Conqueror, is infused with
wonderful pleasure.

Chin P'ing Mei

The reason some women will never be nudists is
that they can never decide what not to wear.

Anonymous

Women never look so well as when one comes in
wet and dirty from hunting.

R. S. Surtees

The odds are usually two-to-one in favor of sex: you
and she against her conscience.

Anonymous

Sex appeal is the mystery behind the mastery of
woman over man.

Anonymous

Beware of the girl with the baby stare – a man is
safer in the electric chair.

Anonymous

I'd like to be that rock she sat on.

James Joyce

Women complain about sex more often than men.
Their gripes fall into two major categories: 1) Not
enough 2) Too much.

Ann Landers

A skirt is no obstacle to extemporaneous sex, but it is physically impossible to make love to a girl while she is wearing trousers.

Helen Lawrenson

I do have big tits. Always had 'em – push 'em up, whack 'em around. Why not make fun of 'em? I've made a fortune with 'em.

Dolly Parton

. . . her friendly bust
gives promise of pneumatic bliss.

T. S. Eliot

You can take the girl out of the cheap underwear, but you can't take the cheap underwear out of the girl.

Anonymous

What a man enjoys about a woman's clothes are his fantasies of how she would look without them.

Brendan Francis

I guess I'm in the bikini-stuffing business.

Pamela Anderson

I dress for women, but I undress for men.

Angie Dickinson

Full nakedness! All joys are due to thee,
As souls unbodied, bodies unclothed must be,
To taste whole joys.
Then since that I may know,
As liberally as a midwife, show

Thyself: cast all, yea, this white linen hence,
There is no penance due to innocence.
To teach thee, I am naked first; why then
What need'st thou have more covering than a man?

John Donne

She wore far too much rogue last night and not
quite enough clothes. That is always a sign of
despair in a woman.

Oscar Wilde

I'm a one-hour mama,
So no one-minute papa
Ain't the kind of man for me.

Porter Granger, song lyric

We, being modern and liberated . . . must never
relax our guard against (man's) chauvinistic sexual
fantasies. So don't even for an instant consider
keeping the following hidden in the back of your
closet: a see-through nurse's uniform . . . a
cheerleader's costume . . . a little black French
maid's outfit.

Cynthia Heimel

The most effective lure that a woman can hold out
to a man is the lure that he fatuously conceives to
be her beauty. This so-called beauty, of course, is
almost always an illusion. The female body, even at
its best, is very defective in form; it has harsh curves
and very clumsily distributed masses; compared to
it the average milk jug or even cuspidor, is a thing
of intelligent and gratifying design.

H. L. Mencken

Some women blush when they are kissed; some call
for the police; some swear; some bite; but the worst
are those who laugh.

Anonymous

In pursuit of my life-long quest for naked women
in wet mackintoshes.

Dylan Thomas,
when asked by a reporter why he'd come to America

She's showing me her clit ring. That's why I have
that expression on my face.

Madonna

If you are a girl, worry that your breasts are too
round . . . or too pointed. If you are a boy, worry
that you will get breasts.

Delia Ephron

I never could dance well. People came to see me
because I was the first who dared to show myself
naked to the public.

Mata Hari

A woman is a well-served table that one sees with
different eyes before and after the meal.

Honore de Balzac

. . . neither hell fire nor the earth being so
devouring as the privy parts of a lascivious woman.

Dr. Nicholas de Venette

The body of a young woman is God's greatest
achievement . . . Of course, He could have built it
to last longer but you can't have everything.

Neil Simon

So the female orgasm . . . may be thought of as a
sort of pleasure prize like a prize that comes with a
box of cereal.

Madeline Gray

The worst lay in the world. She was always drunk
and always eating.

Peter Lawford, talking about Rita Hayworth

There are no good girls gone wrong, just bad girls
found out.

Mae West

The only lover I'm ever gonna need is your soft,
sweet little girl's tongue.

Bruce Springsteen, song lyric

I hope that when people see me in *Playboy*, they'll
see more than the surface.

Pamela Anderson

She always looks like she's just been fucked.

Jason Williams

Every man I know gets an erection just by talking
about her.

Paul Bern, about his wife, Jean Harlow

Of all the world's vistas, the one that cannot be
surpassed is the female posterior.

John B. Keane

So many beautiful women and so little time.

John Barrymore

Isn't it so amazing that these erogenous zones are different for everyone? My biggest erogenous zone happens to be my vagina.

Sarah Silverman

When a man says he had pleasure with a woman he does not mean conversation.

Samuel Johnson

I need a little sugar in my bowl
And a little hot dog between my roll.

Bessie Smith, song lyric

Women whose tongues won't stay in their mouths are the sexiest.

John Updike

All the ugly ones fuck.

Thomas Pynchon

I love my pussy. I think it's the complete summation of my life.

Madonna

. . . 56% of women questioned admitted to becoming aroused while doing their laundry, even at public laundromats . . . Various soap smells seemed to play a role in female arousal.

Dr. Ernest Masfield

She tore off mask after mask –
Wonder Woman
Noble Martyr
Big Mama
Con Woman
Tough Broad
Sexy Kitten
Cold Bitch
Daddy's Girl
Frightened Child
Whiny Brat
and on and on . . .

Nancy Green

He will not manage her, although he mount her.

William Shakespeare

. . . her odalisque lips lusciously smeared with the salve of swine fat and rosewater.

James Joyce

If you would have a hen lay, you must bear with her cackling.

Thomas Fuller

As women have known since the dawn of our time, the primary site for stimulation to orgasm centers on the clitoris. The revolution unleashed by the Kinsey Report of 1953 has, by now, made this information available to men who, for whatever reason, had not figured it out for themselves by the more obvious routes of experience and sensitivity.

Stephen Jay Gould

Wink, wink, nudge, nudge, say no more, know
what I mean?

Eric Idle

God, how I envied girls. Whatever it was on them,
it didn't dangle between their legs like an
elephant trunk.

Julius Lester

If women were more sexual, I'd like them better.

Brittany Andrews

Women have served all these centuries as looking-
glasses possessing the magic and delicious power of
reflecting the figure of man at twice its natural
size.

Virginia Woolf

Wow! It's so BIG!

Sharon Kane, porn actress

If there's one thing about strippers I don't like it's
how their butts always have that metal pole smell.

Sarah Silverman

People will insist on treating the *mons Veneris* as
though it were Mount Everest.

Aldous Huxley

Men do make passes at girls who wear glasses – but
it all depends on their frames.

Optical ad

. . . To sleep carelessly in the shadow of her breasts
Like a peaceful village at the foot of a mountain.

Charles Baudelaire

Men have been trained and conditioned by
women, not unlike the way Pavlov conditioned his
dogs, into becoming their slaves. As compensation
for their labors men are given periodic use of
women's vaginas.

Esther Vilar

I like to have my own way, to lie down mistress and
get up master.

Susanna Moodie

There are two ways to handle a woman, and
nobody knows either of them.

Kin Hubbard

Even if you understood women, you'd never
believe it.

Frank Dane

Women are made to be loved, not understood.

Oscar Wilde

⸗11⸗

Sex Is Good, But Not As Good As Fresh Sweet Corn

Sex is the biggest nothing of all time.

Andy Warhol

After making love I said to my girl, "Was it good for you?" And she said, "I don't think this was good for anybody."

Garry Shandling

I suspect that one of the reasons we create fiction is to make sex exciting.

Gore Vidal

I'd rather hit than have sex.

Reggie Jackson

I tend to believe that cricket is the greatest thing
God ever created on earth . . . certainly greater
than sex, although sex isn't too bad either.

Harold Pinter

Painting and fucking are not compatible.

Vincent Van Gogh

(My mother) thought of sex as some sort of
uncomfortable imposition necessary to continue
the Catholic population.

Linda Lovelace

I just had a pitiful orgasm. It doesn't even qualify as
full-fledged. Let's just call it an org.

Elise D'Haene

He was a real chubby guy – he weighed about 220
pounds – and I've been drawn to chubby guys all
my life since then. . . . It lasted about a minute and
a half. I didn't get off, and I'm going, "This is what
the big deal is about?"

Colleen Brennan, porn actress,
on her introduction to sex

I don't care about sex anymore. It's been years
since I made love. Nowadays I so much prefer
motorcycles.

Mickey Rourke

No Sex Please, We're British.

Play title

Warning signs that your lover is bored: 1)
Passionless kisses. 2) Frequent sighs. 3) Moved, left
no forwarding address.

Matt Groening

We are now all dangerously aware that sexual
intercourse is a bit of a bore. What kept the "divine
woman" lark going all those long, dark centuries
was not an unquenchable erection but romance.

Quentin Crisp

Sex is a momentary itch. Love never lets you go.

Kingsley Amis

Buggery is spiritually valuable because of its
difficulties and torments.

W. H. Auden

After being alive, the next hardest work is sex . . .
Some people get energy from sex, and some
people lose energy from sex. I have found that it's
too much work. But if you have the time for it, and
if you need the exercise – then you should do it.

Andy Warhol

I could be content that we might procreate like
trees, without conjunction, or that there were any
way to perpetuate the world without this trivial and
vulgar way of coition; it is the foolishest act a wise
man commits in all his life.

Thomas Browne

Nothing in our culture, not even home computers,
is more overrated than the epidermal felicity of
two featherless bipeds in desperate congress.

Quentin Crisp

All this fuss about sleeping together. For physical
pleasure I'd sooner go to my dentist any day.

Evelyn Waugh

(Sex is) a perfectly normal, almost commonplace
activity . . . of the same nature as dancing or tennis.

Aldous Huxley

An orgasm is just a reflex like a sneeze.

Dr. Ruth Westheimer

I know it (sex) does make people happy, but to me
it is just like having a cup of tea.

Madam Cynthia Payne

I can resist everything except temptation.

Oscar Wilde

Abstainer: A weak person who yields to the
temptation of denying himself a pleasure.

Ambrose Bierce

After three days men grow weary of a wench, a
guest, and rainy weather.

Benjamin Franklin

Genitals are a great distraction to scholarship.

Malcolm Bradbury

The old-fashioned girl yielded to a man's embrace
as if she were slowly lowering herself into a tub of
cold water.

James Thurber

Continental people have a sex life; the English
have hot-water bottles.

George Mikes

No sex. Sex is the most tiring thing in the world.

Elsa Maxwell

Sex can lead to conception and be as rewarding as
cold piss . . .

Norman Mailer

Orgasmism is a Western neurosis, but I say once
you've had one, you've had them all.

Germaine Greer

I'll probably never have children because I don't
believe in touching people for any reason.

Paula Poundstone

Today, on an Ivy League campus, if a guy tells a girl
she's got great tits, she can charge him with sexual
harassment. Chickenshit stuff. Is this what strong
women do?

Camille Paglia

You have kindergarten harassers. We're reaching
out and identifying them at the earliest grades.

Senator Edward Kennedy

Don't ask me about sex. I know more about carrots.
I suspect it's an acquired taste one can do without.

Hanif Kureishi

Sex is the last refuge of the miserable.

Quentin Crisp

The so-called new morality is the old immorality
condoned.

Lord Shawcross

As soon as one is unhappy one becomes moral.

Marcel Proust

Love is two minutes, fifty-two seconds of squishing
noises.

Johnny Rotten

Sex has never been an obsession with me. It's just
like eating a bag of crisps. Quite nice, but nothing
marvelous.

Boy George

The pleasure is momentary, the position is
ridiculous, and the expense is damnable.

Lord Chesterfield

'Tis the Devil inspires this evanescent ardor, in
order to divert the parties from prayer.

Martin Luther,
founder of the Protestant Church

. . . sexuality remains one of the demonic forces in
human consciousness – pushing us at intervals
close to taboo and dangerous desires . . .

Susan Sontag

Surely the sex business isn't worth all this damned
fuss? I've only met a handful of people who cared a
biscuit for it.

T. E. Lawrence (Lawrence of Arabia)

I love Mickey Mouse more than any woman I've ever known.

Walt Disney

If I have to cry, I think of my sex life. If I have to laugh, I think of my sex life.

Glenda Jackson

I can't move my body. All I can do is press the buzzer at the head of my bed... I tell the night nurse to come back when everyone is asleep. In my state, sex is pretty tricky. But she straddles me so skillfully that my dick stands up despite everything, and she rides me so cautiously that neither her butt nor her vaginal lips so much as graze my abdomen even once. The climax is very painful, so we can do it only once.

Klaus Kinski, from his
autobiography, "I Need Love

In the good old days, you'd get gonorrhea, your dick hurt, you'd go get a shot and clear it right up. Then they came out with herpes. You keep that shit forever, like luggage. And now they got AIDS. That just kills motherfuckers. What's next? I guess you just put your dick in and explode.

Eddie Murphy

. . . your groin and buttocks and thighs ache like hell and you're all wet and bloody and it wasn't like a Hollywood movie at all, but Jesus, at least you're not a virgin anymore – but is that what this is all about? And meanwhile he's asking, "Did you cum?"

Robin Morgan

People always say that the first time hurts, but it
didn't for me. It felt like taking a crap, only out of
my pussy.

Regan Starr

You should read Saint Augustine on this. He said
that in the garden of Eden, before the fall,
reproduction took place in just the same way and
with just the same lack of excitement as one
excretes or passes water.

Alan Watts

It amazes me that organs that piss
Can give human beings such perfect bliss.

Irving Layton

The more sex becomes a non-issue in people's
lives, the happier they are.

Shirley Maclaine

I think sex is dead anyway.

Elizabeth Taylor

When a man is enjoying the gratification of sexual
passion or the pleasure of eating he ought to feel
the presence of poison and be reminded of
original sin.

Nicholas Berdyaev

I've asked the fellows in this hut . . . they all say it's
all over in ten minutes. For myself, I haven't tried
it, and hope not to.

T. E. Lawrence (Lawrence of Arabia)

A man can go seventy years without a piece of ass, but he can die in a week without a bowel movement.

Charles Bukowski

The act of procreation and the members employed therein are so repulsive, that if it were not for the beauty of the faces and the adornments of the actors and the pent-up impulse, nature would lose the human species.

Leonardo Da Vinci

It's really such an odd quirky little exercise. . . . the woman's just about to kiss her own tit, she sees you looking at her . . . she realizes you're no longer in the throes of it. She tries to smooth things out, but she knows you've caught her. And she looks at you and says, "If you ever mention it, I'll kill you in your sleep, you treacherous cocksucker." And that is sex, so leave it at that and don't even try to figure it out.

Dennis Miller

The perfect lover is one who turns into a pizza at 4 a.m.

Charles Pierce

Sex is good, but not as good as fresh sweet corn.

Garrison Keillor

⸗12⸗

What Do I Know About Sex?
I'm A Married Man

No man should marry until he has studied anatomy and dissected at least one woman.

Honore de Balzac

Lovers need to explore more than each other's bodies. They need to plunge into each other's psyches and soar to the heights of the spirit.

Nik Douglas and Penny Slinger

Splendid couple – slept with both of them.

Sir Maurice Bowra

A man can have two, maybe three, love affairs while he's married. After that it's cheating.

Yves Montand

Marriage is like a bank account. You put it in, you take it out, you lose interest.

Professor Irwin Corey

I wouldn't trust my husband with a young woman for five minutes, and he's been dead for 25 years.

Brendan Behan's mother

Road signs hold the wisdom of the universe:
SOFT SHOULDERS
DANGEROUS CURVES
MERGING TRAFFIC
MEN AT WORK
LOOK OUT FOR CHILDREN

If monogamy is the height of all virtue then the palm goes to the tapeworm, which has a complete set of male and female sexual organs . . . and spends its whole life copulating . . . with itself.

Friedrich Engels

It has been my experience that folks who have no vices have very few virtues.

Abraham Lincoln

You want to make your wife scream during sex? You wipe your dick on the curtains.

Rodney Dangerfield

If you were half a man – and you are.

Overheard marital dispute

I suspected that my husband has been fooling around. When I confronted him with the evidence

he denied everything and said it would never
happen again.

Letter to Dear Abby

My wife has cut our love-making down to once a
month, but I know two guys she's cut out entirely.

Rodney Dangerfield

I couldn't stand that my husband was unfaithful. I
am Raquel Welch – understand?

Raquel Welch

If you were married to Marilyn Monroe you'd
cheat with some ugly girl.

George Burns

You mustn't force sex to do the work of love or love
to do the work of sex.

Mary McCarthy

Remember when you figured out that your parents
must have done it? Alright, once for me, once for
my brother. That's it.

Lana Holstein, MD

My parents never had sex.

D. B. Hammond

(After intercourse) dancing about the room
before repose, for a few minutes, might probably
have that effect (of preventing conception), but
trotting a horse briskly over a rough road on the
following day would ensure it.

Eugene Becklard, M.D., in
"Becklard's Physiology," 1845

To my embarrassment I was born in bed with a lady.
Wilson Mizner

Adultery: second only to front-line combat,
produces feats of almost lunatic daring. And it
thrives on the extraordinary capacity of the
deceived partner to ignore signs of infidelity, so
obvious to the rest of the world.
Mary Beard

You have to accept the fact that part of the sizzle of
sex comes from the danger of sex.
Camille Paglia

Unfortunately, this world is full of people who are
ready to think the worst when they see a man
sneaking out of the wrong bedroom in the middle
of the night.
Will Cuppy

The main thing in marriage is that, for a man, sex
is a hunger – like eating. If a man is hungry and
can't get to a fancy French restaurant, he'll go to a
hotdog stand. For a woman, what's important is
love and romance.
Joan Fontaine

My beloved, man of my choice,
May you put your right hand in my vulva,
With your left stretched towards my head,
When you have neared your mouth to my mouth,
When you have taken my lips into your mouth,
Thus you swear the oath to me.
Sumerian wedding song

A diaphragm is like a shower cap for cats. By the
time you get it in, your kids are in college.

Suzy Sorra

The other night I said to my wife, Ruth, "Do you
feel that the sex and excitement has gone out of
our marriage?" Ruth said, "I'll discuss it with you
during the next commercial."

Milton Berle

Last time I tried to make love to my wife nothing
was happening. So I said to her, "What's the
matter, you can't think of anybody either?"

Rodney Dangerfield

Marriage was a woman's idea: Let me get this
straight, honey. I can't sleep with anyone else for
the rest of my life, and if things don't work out,
you get to keep half of my stuff? What a great idea!

Bobby Slayton

My heart has made its mind up
And I'm afraid it's you.

Wendy Cope

Brides aren't happy – they are just triumphant.

John Barrymore

Kissing don't last: cookery do!

George Meredith

Marriage is popular because it combines the maximum of temptation with the maximum of opportunity.

George Bernard Shaw

A husband is what is left of a lover, after the nerve has been extracted.

Helen Rowland

God made him, and therefore let him pass as a man.

William Shakespeare

Literature is mostly about sex and not much about having children and life is the other way round.

David Lodge

I wonder if I really satisfied her during our seven year marriage, or if she was faking that night?

Woody Allen

They say if you put a penny in a jar every time you have sex during your first year of marriage, then take out a penny every time you have sex the rest of the years you're married, the jar will never be empty.

Howard Edgar

Sex drive: A physical craving that begins in adolescence and ends at marriage.

Robert Byrne

Never Kiss a Married Woman on the Thigh.

Shel Silverstein, song title

I've been married for six years and have five kids.
My husband still wants to have sex every night and
sometimes in the morning, too. I told him he
should get himself a hobby. He says that sex is his
hobby.

Letter to Dear Abby

Marriage (whether registered or not) begins, not
with setting up house, counting wedding presents,
blowing kisses, looking at wedding groups, but with
two bodies confronting one another like two
wrestlers. To clinch and struggle and contend with
one another. Rolling about, now one on top, now
another; grunting, croaking, sweating, murmuring,
yelling. So the world began, with vast turbulence in
the genitalia of space.

Malcolm Muggeridge

The ideal that marriage aims at is that of spiritual
union through the physical. The human love that
it incarnates is intended to serve as a stepping-
stone to divine or universal love.

Mohandas Gandhi

The way to a man's heart is through his wife's belly,
and don't you forget it.

Edward Albee

I've only slept with men I've been married to. How
many women can make that claim?

Elizabeth Taylor

Much contention and strife will arise in that house
where the wife shall get up dissatisfied with her
husband.

Sa'di

The best sex education for kids is when Daddy pats Mommy on the fanny when he comes home from work.

Dr. William H. Masters

It's far more important to find someone to sleep next to than it is to find someone to sleep with. Because you have to trust the person you're sleeping next to.

Viper

Before she said "I do" . . . she did.

Bill Margold

I think the people who like sex stay home. I mean I don't think they make a big thing out of it.

Nelson Algren

Marriage is the price men pay for sex; sex is the price women pay for marriage.

Anonymous

A mutual sexual attraction is no proper basis for a human relationship . . .

John MacMurray

The greatest illusion of lovers is to believe that the intensity of their sexual attraction is the guarantee of the perpetuity of their love.

Bishop Fulton J. Sheen

I think, therefore I'm single.

Liz Winston

I wish I would have known how creative, consistent and ongoing sex would have to be.

Maria Shriver, writing about her marriage

Once, while we were making love, a curious optical illusion occurred, and it almost looked as though she were moving.

Woody Allen

No chupa, no shtupa. (Translation: No wedding, no bedding.)

Yiddish proverb

. . . she'd been bored stiff with me and I bored limp with her . . .

John Barth

A wholesome sexual relationship changes with marriage because all of a sudden you're sleeping with a relative.

Andrew Ward

A man marries to have a home, but also because he doesn't want to be bothered with sex and all that sort of thing.

Somerset Maugham

Let not the fear of bad offspring deter you. . . . You do your duty.

Hammuna, Talmud: Berakot

There is absolutely nothing loving about sex. Lust is as destructive inside of marriage as it is outside.

Father John McGoey

Studies in which men and women are asked to
rank their pleasures in order of enjoyment show
repeatedly that whereas sex is the favorite for most
men, many women prefer knitting.

Dr. Glenn Wilson

Dear Abby:
Are birth control pills tax deductible?

Kay

Dear Kay:
Only if they don't work.

Abby

Husbands would never go whoring
They would stay with the ones they adore
If wives were but half alluring
After the act as before.

The Greek Anthology

I wasn't kissing her, I was just whispering in her
mouth.

Chico Marx,
on being caught with a chorus girl by his wife

"Goodsex" — that is to say, normal intercourse
between man and wife, for the sole purpose of
begetting children, and without physical pleasure
on the part of the woman; all else was "sexcrime."
George Orwell, in the novel "Nineteen Eighty-Four"

What men call gallantry, and gods adultry,
Is much more common where the climate's sultry.
Lord Byron

Cease hunting married game: trouble and grief
more often come to you than real enjoyment.

Horace

When I walked in on my wife and the milkman,
the first thing she said is, "Don't tell the butcher."

Rodney Dangerfield

Monogamous is what one partner in every
relationship wants to be.

Anonymous

Married love is a creative enterprise. . . .
Perfunctory coitus is a confession of lack of
intelligence and character.

Alexis Carrel

Her exotic daydreams do not prevent her from
being small-town bourgeois at heart . . . adultery
being the most conventional way to rise above the
conventional.

Vladimir Nabokov

The number of affairs a man has after his marriage
is probably equal to the number he didn't have
before it.

Richard J. Needham

Here's to our wives and lovers – may they never
meet!

Anonymous

The bed: A place where marriages are decided.

Anonymous

Nowadays all married men live like bachelors, all bachelors live like married men.

Oscar Wilde

I was in love once when I was young. But then I became attached to the Bureau.

J. Edgar Hoover

I feel like Zsa Zsa Gabor's fifth husband. I know what I'm supposed to do, but I don't know if I can make it interesting.

Vice President Al Gore

Never have your wife in the morning – the day may have something better to offer.

P.V. Taylor

I could not abide marriage, but as a rambler, I took a snatch when I could get it.

Robert Burton

Peter (Gabriel) and I had a very big affair for many years, and it was very painful for a lot of people – including his wife.

Rosanna Arquette

How many husbands have I had? You mean apart from my own?

Zsa Zsa Gabor

The prerequisite for a good marriage is the license to be unfaithful.

Carl Jung

I don't screw around. I wish I had.

Dan Rather

I'd like to get married because I like the idea of a man being required by law to sleep with me every night.

Carrie Snow

Sex in marriage is like medicine. Three times a day for the first week. Then once a day for another week. Then once every three or four days until the condition clears up.

Peter DeVries

There is one thing I would break up over, and that is if she caught me with another woman. I won't stand for that.

Steve Martin

Matrimony is the only state under which every man is free to choose his own form of government: blonde, brunette or redhead.

Anonymous

Virginity is preferable to marriage.

Pope Pius XII

My husband complained to me, he said, "I can't remember when we last had sex," and I said, "Well, I can and that's why we ain't doing it."

Roseanne Barr

Before children ever get to school they will have received crucial, almost irrevocable sex education

and this will have been taught by the parents, who
are not aware of what they are doing.

Dr. Mary S. Calderone

Sex is dirty and filthy. Save it for someone you love.

Anonymous

When things don't work well in the bedroom, they
don't work well in the living room either.

Dr. William H. Masters

Love consists in regarding your own much as little,
and your Beloved's little as much.

Ba-Yazid Bistami

The Biblical revelation . . . does not limit the
function of sexuality and the family to the
reproductive purpose. Equally deeply rooted in
Genesis is the reflection of a second factor – the
need of man and woman for each other, to
complement and fulfill each other and to establish
a durable partnership against the loneliness and
rigor of life.

Lambeth Conference of Anglican Bishops, 1958

Sexuality is the last frontier in relationships. Who
tells you how to have more nourishing sexual
relationships?

Lana Holstein, MD

It is now lawful for a Catholic woman to avoid
pregnancy by a resort to mathematics, though she
is still forbidden to resort to physics and chemistry.

H. L. Mencken

Family Planning – Use rear entrance.
Sign at a Family Planning Clinic

The best contraception is a glass of cold water: not
before or after, but instead.
*Pakistani delegate to an
International Planned Parenthood conference*

Postumus, are you really taking a wife? Isn't it
better to sleep with a pretty boy? Boys don't
quarrel all night, or nag you for little presents
while they're on the job, or complain that you
don't come up to their expectations, or demand
more gasping passion.
Juvenal

She could commit adultery at one end and weep
for her sins at the other, and enjoy both operations
at the same time.
Joyce Cary

A brief history of sex in marriage: naked . . . satin
and silk . . . combed cotton . . . old flannel.
John-Paul Sousa

When it comes to love, no one is loyal anymore.
Propertius, Roman poet, circa 50-15 BCE

If there were more than two, it would not be Eden.
It is the impossibility of intrusion that makes it
Eden. Into the true Eden there is a certain
impossibility of intrusion. This is a true marriage.
John S. Bayne

What do I know about sex? I'm a married man.
Tom Clancy

=13=

Though I Look Old, Yet I Am Strong And Lusty

You're only as old as the woman you feel.

Groucho Marx

I remember giving blowjobs, it's just that I don't remember to whom I've given them.

Juliet Anderson, retired porn star, at age 63

I have everything now I had twenty years ago – except it's all lower.

Gypsy Rose Lee

You may be certain that age is galloping upon you when . . . a feminine voice over the telephone says, "Do you know who this is?" And you say, "No," and hang up the receiver.

Franklin Pierce Adams

When you're over 90, having sex is like shooting
pool with a rope.

George Burns

As I grow older and older,
And totter towards the tomb,
I find that I care less and less
Who goes to bed with whom.

Dorothy L. Sayers

The most distressing fact of growing older is that I
find my private parts shrinking.

Cecil Beaton

Ah! If only I could say the same.

Greta Garbo

She's 100, but she's wearing something tight.

Leonard Cohen, song lyric

Is it not strange that desire should so many years
outlive performance?

William Shakespeare

The middle age of buggers is not to be
contemplated without horror.

Virginia Woolf

As a young man I used to have four supple
members and one stiff one. Now I have four stiff
and one supple.

Henri, Duc D'Aumale

Chastity is not chastity in an old man, but a
disability to be unchaste.

John Donne

Older women are best because they always think
they may be doing it for the last time.

Ian Fleming

. . . as in the dark all cats are grey, the pleasure of
corporeal enjoyment with an old woman is at least
equal, and frequently superior, every knack being
by practice capable of improvement.

Benjamin Franklin

At age 82, I sometimes feel like a twenty-year-old,
but there is seldom one around.

Milton Berle

There goes a saying, and 'twas shrewdly said,
Old fish at the table, but young flesh in bed.

Alexander Pope

The great thing about being thirty is that . . . the
young women look younger and the old one's
don't look nearly so old.

Glen Frey

You'll have to ask somebody older than me.

Eubie Blake, at 96,
when asked at what age interest in sex fades

Someone asked Sophocles, "How do you feel now
about sex? Are you still able to have a woman?" He
replied, "Hush, man; most glad indeed I am to be

rid of it all, as though I had escaped from a mad
and savage master.

Plato

Regarding what is below the girdle, it is impossible
of two women to know an old one from a young
one.

Benjamin Franklin

Because it takes forty years to get rid of the
puritanical bullshit that's in our culture!

*Suzi Wahl, asked why some people
enjoy sex more at middle-age*

If the young only knew; if the old only could.

French proverb

No man knows what true happiness is until he has
a complete set of false teeth and has lost all
interest in the opposite sex.

Lord Rosebery

No one is too old for some things.

Martial

Though I look old, yet I am strong and lusty.

William Shakespeare

=14=

Nobody Ever Died
From An Overdose Of Pornography

Pornography is in the groin of the beholder.

Charles Rembar

The difference between pornography and erotica is lighting.

Gloria Leonard

Yes, I'd pose nude for the money, to boost my ego, and to prove real women are the only option. However, I would refuse to pose while eating bananas or any other phallic-related symbols, and I don't really fancy the idea of sticking my butt skyrocketing high up in the air. I was more thinking about posing nude while neurotically trying to put on my jeans that did fit only last year, desperately

trying to remove all hair-related obstacles on my
body, and lazily hanging in front of the TV wearing
unbecoming slippers.

Monique Menke

Since the human body is the most perfect of all
forms, we cannot see it too often.

Kenneth Clark

There's only one good test of pornography. Get
twelve normal men to read the book, and then ask
them, "Did you get an erection?" If the answer is
"Yes" from a majority of the twelve, then the book
is pornographic.

W. H. Auden

The test that suppresses a cheap tract today can
suppress a literary gem tomorrow. All it need do is
incite a lascivious thought or arouse a lustful
desire. The list of books that judges or juries can
place in that category is endless.

William O. Douglas, Supreme Court Justice

What's wrong with appealing to prurient interest?
We appeal to killing interest.

Lenny Bruce

After three years of intensive research, the
National Commission on Obscenity and
Pornography (appointed by President Lyndon
Johnson in 1967) found no evidence that
pornography was harmful; the real problem, it said
in its 1970 report, was "the inability or reluctance
of people in our society to be open and direct in
dealing with sexual matters."

Marjorie Heins

Allowing for its crudities, the sexual revolution has been one of the few blessings in the life of this century.

V. S. Pritchett

In Catholic sexual morality, the deliberate arousal of sexual thoughts . . . is of itself a serious sin.

Harold C. Gardiner

The first thing that strikes one about American female porn stars is that almost all of them seem to hail from rather conservative family backgrounds and were subject to very strict religious upbringing.

Phyllis and Eberhard Kronhausen
in "The Sex People"

I had a crazy uncle who believed that every word of the Bible was literally true, including the marginal notes. Until one day he was reading a passage in the Book of Proverbs and found a naughty word in the Bible. And from that time on, he was through with it. I mean, how Protestant can you get?

Alan Watts

Having sex for a porn star is just like shaking hands.

Bill Margold, from "The Porn Stud Handbook"

He didn't realize how hard it was until he found out how soft it was.

Candy Samples, explaining her boyfriend's attempt
to perform with her in porn films

When we climaxed, everyone clapped.

Tina Russell, on acting in her first porn film

I've seen "Deep Throat" about seven or eight times now and I enjoy watching myself. To tell the truth it makes me kind of horny.

Linda Lovelace

Now, some of the guys on the set say, "Hey, far out, baby, why don't you come home with me . . ." But this is where it stops, as far as I'm concerned. There's got to be the same kind of professionalism as in any other kind of acting.

Marilyn Chambers

I'm just thinking about my fuckin' Dad renting this and then some dude's got his dick bouncing on my nose and I'm blowing bubbles and shit. It's fuckin' hilarious.

Daisy, in her first porn scene with Rodney Moore

It's a bawdy planet.

William Shakespeare

So I can have sex with 10,000 men at one time rather than just one.

Viper, asked why she became a porn star

The X-rated industry is a juvenile hall where recess is 24 hours a day and the bell of responsibility never rings.

Bill Margold

Maybe I'll make a "Mary Poppins" movie and shove the umbrella up my ass.

Marilyn Chambers

My reaction to porno films is as follows: After the first ten minutes, I want to go home and screw. After the first twenty minutes, I never want to screw anything as long as I live.

Erica Jong

To have to make love without feeling a particle is sad work . . .

Henry Edward Fox

If sex is such a natural phenomenon, how come there are so many books on how to?

Bette Midler

We have long passed the Victorian era when asterisks were followed at a certain interval by a baby.

Somerset Maugham

Is nakedness indecent? No, not inherently so. It is your thought, your sophistication, your fear, your respectability, that is indecent. There come moods when these clothes of ours are not only irksome to wear, but are themselves indecent.

Walt Whitman

We are not taught to think decently on sex subjects, and consequently we have no language for them except indecent language.

Bernard Shaw

What is pornography to one man may be the
laughter of genius to another.

D. H. Lawrence

Erotic realism is a . . . rebellion against social
pressures to deny and falsify life by forcing (artists
and writers) to exclude, minimize and distort the
sexual element in (their) artistic creation. . . .
Erotic realism's only goal is to depict life as it is.

Eberhard and Phyllis Kronhausen

Love is just a four-letter word.

Bob Dylan

A dirty book is seldom a dusty one.

Anonymous

. . . physical gratification will no longer be
regarded as any more indecent than the appetites
of the other senses: the love of feasts, concerts,
perfumes, finery, etc.

Charles Fourier

The Internet is bestiality, pedophilia, child
molestation . . . one quarter of all the images
involve the torture of women.

Ralph Reed, Christian Coalition leader

The religious right sees sexuality as an external
force, a threat . . . Fashion ads. Rap music. Sex
education. Videos. Once you believe sex is an
outside force, you look for it everywhere – which is
a textbook definition of paranoia.

Marty Klein

I know they'd rather have kids learn about sex the same way they did – from disgraced TV evangelists. . . . But abstinence isn't working for priests these days, so I doubt it's going to work for teenagers . . .

Dennis Miller

Some women . . . actually thrill to the threat of physical violence. I've never met one that does, but they probably do exist. In books. By men.

Alan Ayckbourn

Women tend not to dress up in leather aprons and nail each other to coffee tables in their spare time.

Julie Burchill

Rushing consisted mostly of inviting potential pledges to smokers while we drank beer and watched pornographic movies. The movies, in the sexually repressed Fifties, were supposed to be a draw. I hooted and hollered with the rest of the college boys through these grainy eight-millimeter films, in which the male star usually wore socks.

Colin Powell

Women really run the porn industry. They make the most money. It's the opposite in the rest of the world. Prostitution and stripping are direct forms of whoring, while almost every other job is an indirect form.

Sarah Silverman

It's only at airports and railway stations that one finds in oneself a curiosity about . . . girlie magazines.

Tom Stoppard

I'm not against naked girls – not as often as I'd like to be.

Benny Hill

. . . when you're a kid you use the pornographic playing cards as a substitute for a real experience, and when you're older you use real experience as a substitute for fantasy.

Edward Albee

It's a sad day for sexual liberation when the pornography addict has to settle for the real thing.

Brendan Francis

A word about pornography. You'll need it. Lots of it. The dirty, filthy, degrading kind. But keep it well hidden. Especially if you have teenage boys or a Baptist wife.

John Hughes

I think naked people are very nice. Posing in the nude is perhaps the best way of reaching people.

Stella Stevens

. . . half the business world is juiced by the sort of half-sex that one finds in advertisements.

Norman Mailer

If a man is pictured chopping off a woman's breast, it only gets an "R" rating. But if, God forbid, a man

is pictured kissing a woman's breast, it gets an "X"
rating. Why is violence more acceptable than
tenderness?"

Sally Struthers

The pornography of violence of course far
exceeds, in volume and general acceptance, sexual
pornography, in this Puritan land of ours. . . . For
the ultimate selling job on ultimate violence one
must read those works of fiction issued by our
government . . .

Ursula K. LeGuin

Those Romans who perpetrated the rape of the
Sabines, for example, did not work themselves up
for the deed by screening "Debbie Does Dallas,"
and the monkish types who burned a million or so
witches in the Middle Ages had almost certainly
not come across "Boobs and Buns" or related
periodicals.

Barbara Ehrenreich

The only thing pornography has been known to
cause is solitary masturbation.

Gore Vidal

The message of pornography, by its very existence,
is that our sexual selves are real.

Sallie Tisdale

I would like to see all people who read
pornography, or have anything to do with it, put in
a mental hospital . . .

Linda Lovelace, former porn star

I've got an idea! Let's fill the whole screen with
tits.
Hunt Strombert, film producer

Her book about the money in sex gives you the
feeling of the sex in money.
*Leon Wieseltier, on Sydney Biddle Barrows
(aka The Mayflower Madam)*

Diamonds, high finance, and convulsive sex are
crammed into thick books like so much mint
cream into imported chocolates.
Claudia Rosett, on romance novels

Pornography is the quadrophonics of sex.
Jean Baudrillard

Murder is a crime. Describing murder is not. Sex is
not a crime. Describing sex is.
Gershon Legman

Nobody ever died from an overdose of
pornography.
Bill Margold

=15=

Censorship Is The Strongest Drive In Human Nature; Sex Is A Weak Second.

Pontius Pilate was the first great censor, and Jesus Christ the first great victim of censorship.

Ben Lindsay

(Julia) had grasped the inner meaning of the Party's sexual Puritanism. It was not merely that the sex instinct created a world of its own which was outside the Party's control and which therefore had to be destroyed if possible. What was more important was that sexual privation induced hysteria, which was desirable because it could be transformed into war fever and leader worship.

George Orwell, in the novel "Nineteen Eighty-Four"

(Erotic literature is) a moral vulture which steals upon our youth, silently striking its terrible talons into their vitals, and forcibly bearing them away on hideous wings to shame and death.

Anthony Comstock

Some of my plays were for many years under the ban of censorship for their obscenity, and they are now disparaged as old-fashion and prudish.

George Bernard Shaw

It's only a big deal in America. Around the world boobs are boobs.

Halle Berry,
on the hype surrounding her first nude scene on film

Most churches in America and in England are, frankly, sexual regulation societies. They occasionally get excited about other moral issues, but really not very much. . . . On the whole sex is sin and sex is dirt.

Alan Watts

Whatever you say, say nothing
When you talk about you-know-what . . .
You all know what I'm speaking of
When I mention you-know-what
And I fear it's very dangerous to even mention that.

Colm Sands, song lyric

All the things I really want to do are either
immoral, illegal or fattening.

Alexander Woollcott

It will allow you and your family to walk without
fear of being offended, or worse, physically
attacked by nude or partially nude persons.

Statement from The American Family Association
on the passing of an ordinance
banning nude sunbathing

Sex . . . has become a national disease. The way we
get it into our politics and religion, where it does
not belong . . .

William Faulkner

Puritanism: The haunting fear that someone,
somewhere, may be happy.

H. L. Mencken

It is the duty of the courts to be watchful for the
constitutional rights of the citizens, and against any
stealthy encroachments thereon. While it is
"obscenity and indecency" before us today, the
experience of mankind – both ancient and
modern – shows that this type of elastic phrase can,
and most likely will, be synonymous with the
political, and maybe with the religious,
unorthodoxy of tomorrow. Censorship is the deadly
enemy of freedom and progress.

Hugo L. Black, Supreme Court Justice

We cannot pass laws to make anything and
everything that might be unethical or immoral a
crime and enforceable by law and prison. We are,

and remain, a free country . . . So what is the
answer? Our answer has always been the positive
alternative!

Reverend Robert H. Schuller

Nature has made union between the sexes the
condition of our existence . . . Why then do we
conceal it like an infraction or a crime?

Alcide Bonneau

There is no way of making a hedge grow like
pruning it. There is no way of making sex
interesting like repressing it.

Alan Watts

I've got nothing against sex, it's a marvelous
human activity, but it was watching others do it all
the time that got me down.

John Trevelyan, British film censor

It's red hot. I hate to think of this sort of book
getting into the wrong hands. As soon as I've
finished this, I shall recommend they ban it.

Tony Hancock

Can we get through this interview without you
using naughty words?

Craig Kilborn

Fuck, no!

Mira Sorvino

Obscenity is whatever happens to shock some
elderly and ignorant magistrate.

Bertrand Russell

The censor believes that he can hold back the
mighty traffic of life with a tin whistle and a raised
right hand. For after all, it is life with which he
quarrels.

Heywood Broun

A controversial exhibit at the Brooklyn Museum of
Art shows the Last Supper with Jesus portrayed as a
naked woman. Mayor Rudolph Guilliani said, "This
trash is not the sort of thing I want to look at when
I go to the museum with my mistress."

Tina Fey, on "Saturday Night Live"

The English public takes no interest in a work of
art until it is told that the work in question is
immoral.

Oscar Wilde

Litigation takes the place of sex at middle age.

Gore Vidal

When it comes to denouncing sexual license, it is
safe for all of us to mount the bandwagon. Still
more profitably, perhaps, we may keep in mind
the occasions when Christ our Lord refused to
mount it.

Alfred Graham

Sexual matters should not be seen as the only
gauge of morality, since Jesus had far greater
concerns, and counted prostitutes among his
closest friends.

Donald Spoto

What progress we are making. In the Middle Ages
they would have burned me; nowadays they are
content with burning my books.

Sigmund Freud

Wherever books are burned, sooner or later men
are also burned.

Heinrich Heine

Sex and obscenity are not synonymous.

William J. Brennan, Supreme Court Justice

Anatomy of an Obscenity Prosecution or, Acts of
Terrorism Against the First Amendment.

Attorney Clyde DeWitt, title of magazine article

The pagans and . . . the feminists and the gays and
the lesbians . . . the ACLU, People for the
American Way, all of them who have tried to
secularize America, I point the finger in their face
and say, "You helped this happen."

Evangelist Jerry Falwell,
reacting to the terrorist attack
on the World Trade Towers in New York City
that killed thousands on September 11, 2001

We become mad in pursuit of sex: we become
equally mad in the persecution of that pursuit.

George Bernard Shaw

People who want to censor sexual material really
want to restrict most of your personal freedoms.
Sex is just one manifestation of what their grasping
hands can't control.

John-Paul Sousa

The most common objection raised by opponents of the Harry Potter books is the way Harry and his friends use magic.

Associated Press report on the restriction and removal of the popular Harry Potter children's books from libraries in 19 states

Many supposedly innocuous popular novels and plays are far more toxic and censorable than the so-called pornographic paperbacks or the lowly comic strip.

Amos N. Wilder

(TV shows like Miami Vice are) the most harmful form of pornography.

Alan Sears,
legal counsel of Citizens for Decency Through Law

... vices which corrupt the heart and moral life should be diligently repressed by public authority, lest they insidiously work the ruin of the State.

Pope Leo XIII, remarks on human liberty, 1888

Are we to have a censor whose imprimatur shall say what books may be sold and what we may buy? Is a priest to be our inquisitor? It is an insult to our citizens . . . For God's sake let us hear both sides if we choose.

President Thomas Jefferson

Censorship can't eliminate evil; it can only kill freedom.

Garrison Keillor

Would-be censors may think that it is the role of
the library to support certain values and causes –
which are, of course, their values and causes.
Intellectual Freedom Manual
of the American Library Association

And the first rude sketch that the world had seen
was joy to Adam's mighty heart
Till the Devil whispered behind the leaves:
"It's pretty, but is it art?"
Rudyard Kipling

(Censorship for) fear of corrupting the mind of
the younger generation is the loftiest form of
cowardice.
Holbrook Jackson

Censorship is the commonest social blasphemy
because it is mostly concealed, built into us by
indolence, self-interest, and cowardice.
John Osborne

I get off on sex as a pleasurable experience. But
for most of the censors, the primary response to
sex is anger. They get off on the anger. That's why
they have a vested interest in keeping women as
victims and viewing porn as rape. . . . It feeds their
anger.
Veronica Vera

And if obscenity law cannot be drafted as neatly as
a speed-limit law, one ought not to complain
excessively.
James J. Kilpatrick

Sex is. There is nothing more to be done about it.
Gore Vidal

Don't join the book burners. Don't think you're
going to conceal faults by concealing evidence that
they ever existed.
President Dwight D. Eisenhower

The First Amendment allows all ideas to be
expressed whether orthodox, popular, off-beat, or
repulsive. . . . We have no business acting as censors
or endowing any group with censorship powers. It
is shocking to me for us to send to prison anyone
for publishing anything.
William O. Douglas, Supreme Court Justice

The artist and the censor differ in this way: the first
is a decent mind in an indecent body and the
second is an indecent mind in a decent body.
George Jean Nathan

Give me six lines written by the most honorable of
men, and I will find an excuse in them to hang
him.
Cardinal Richelieu

The experts agree. Censorship works.
Ad campaign featuring photos of
Joseph Stalin, Adolph Hitler,
Mao Tse-Tung, and Ayatollah Khomeini

Freedom cannot be censored into existence.
President Dwight D. Eisenhower

. . . one must completely ignore (the censor's) hypocritical pretext, and see what should be obvious to a child, that censorship is a political issue, with sex as a simple and shameless pretext.

Pier Paolo Pasolini

The film is apparently meaningless, but if it has any meaning it is doubtless objectionable.

British Board of Film Censors on their
1956 banning of Jean Cocteau's
"The Seashell and The Clergyman."

They can't censor the gleam in my eye.

Charles Laughton

. . . it may be doubted whether it (lust) does as much harm in the world day by day as the less socially disreputable misdemeanors of anger and envy.

Alfred Graham

We all know that books burn – yet we have the greater knowledge that books can not be killed by fire.

President Franklin D. Roosevelt

They that can give up essential liberty to obtain a little temporary safety deserve neither liberty nor safety.

Benjamin Franklin

Censorship is the strongest drive in human nature; sex is a weak second.

Phil Kerby, former editor of the Los Angeles Times

⸗16⸗

The Sexual Embrace Can Only Be Compared With Music And With Prayer

And some to Mecca turn to pray, and I toward thy bed, Yasmin.

James Elroy Flecker

Making love? It's a communion with a woman. The bed is the holy table. There I find passion – and purification.

Omar Sharif

. . . exalting the powers of love will kindle the fires of romance and offer playful and profound ways to contact the divine through earthly love.

Rafael Lorenzo

You have opened up the prison gates of my
womanhood. And all the passion that was
unsatisfied in me for so many years, leaped into a
wild reckless storm boundless as the sea.

Emma Goldman

The appeal of beauty to passion and passion to
beauty was not intended to be a short-lived or
limited thing, but to make life last and to last for
life. Our sex life ought to be a perpetual fountain
of purity and health diffusing its vitality and
fragrance through our whole being.

John S. Bayne

When sex is an expression of love . . . the emotion
experienced at the moment of orgasm is not
hostility or triumph, but union with the other
person . . . it is a giving of one's self and a finding
of one's self at once.

Rollo May

The sex organ is that organ by which
communication is established between man and
the creative force, the manifestation of the divine
being.

Alain Daniélou

Sex lies at the root of life, and we can never learn
to reverence life until we know how to understand
sex.

Havelock Ellis

Nature is to be reverenced, not blushed at.

Tertullian, c. 209

The world seems more cheerful if, when we wake up in the morning, we find we are no longer alone and that there is another human being beside us in the half-dark. That's more cheerful than shelves of edifying books and the white-washed walls of a church.

Vincent Van Gogh

The language of love and desire as ordinary language becomes a language of mystical union, a language of worshipful adoration, a language of spiritual ritual and invocation.

Raphael Lorenzo

My heart craves the kiss of your love, my soul thirsts for the most intimate embrace joining me to you.

Saint Gertrude

Sex is a holy thing, and is one of the most marvelous revelations of the divine.

Alan Watts

In the beginning the first male and the first female stood on the rainbow bridge of heaven and watched the lightning lance thrust down into the waters of chaos. The foam around the jeweled lance solidified to become the first island. Soon the first male and the first female learned how to imitate the act of creation with their own bodies, and from them came the whole world.

The act of creation in Japanese mythology

I valued sexual experience because of its power of producing a celestial flood of emotion and exaltation which, however momentary, gave me a sample of the ecstasy that may one day be the normal condition of conscious intellectual activity.

George Bernard Shaw

Sexual intercourse is in its nature the most perfect method of "laying on of hands" and under proper circumstances may be the most powerful external agency of communicating life to the body, and even the spirit of God to the mind and heart.

J. H. Noyes,
leader in the Utopian religious movement in America

Sex energy is the creative energy of all geniuses.

Napoleon Hill

There is a direct relationship between the highest mental and psychic powers in mankind and the secretions of the sex glands.

Tibetan Book of the Great Liberation

. . . pleasure does not prove that the sexual act conflicts with virtue.

Saint Thomas Aquinas

Sex energy is the root of which love is the flower. . . . We cannot injure the root or reduce its vitality without injuring the flowers.

John S. Bayne

My own view, for what it's worth, is that sexuality is lovely, there cannot be too much of it, it is self-limiting if it is satisfactory, and satisfaction

diminishes tension and clears the mind for
attention and learning.

Paul Goodman

One arousal and the ears and eyes are sharp and bright.
Two arousals and the voice becomes clear.
Three arousals and the skin becomes radiant.
Four arousals and the backbone becomes strong.
Five arousals and the buttocks become muscular.
Six arousals and the water course flows.
Seven arousals and one becomes stout and strong.
Eight arousals and the will is magnified and
  expanded.
Nine arousals and one follows the glory of heaven.
Ten arousals and one manifests spiritual
  illumination.

Chinese Sexual Yoga

The true feeling of sex is that of a deep intimacy,
but above all of a deep complicity.

James Dickey

Love is sacred, and sex is sacred, too. The two
things are not apart; they belong together.

Lame Deer, Lakota Indian holy man

What holds the world together, I have learned
from bitter experience, is sexual intercourse.

Henry Miller

Sex is one instinct of man which can still make us
experience a kind of near-mystical ecstasy. Sex is
more than a biological necessity for propagation of
species: it is also a spiritual need . . .

Trailok Chandra Majupuria

The act of love is a meditation on the great life force.

Mantak Chia

Only through sexual union are new beings capable of existing. This union, therefore, represents a place between two worlds, a point of contact between being and nonbeing, where life manifests itself and incarnates the divine spirit.

Alain Daniélou

I would say the sexual organs express the human soul more than any other limb of the body. They are not diplomats. They tell the truth ruthlessly.

Isaac Bashevis Singer

Judaism does not regard sexual union as a concession to the flesh but at a proper and sacred act.

Arthur Hertzberg

And when is it that man is called one? When man and woman are joined together sexually.

The Zohar

The human need for love and sex is made to bear the burden of all our bodily starvation for contact and sensation, all our creative starvation, all our need for social contact, and even our need to find some meaning in our lives.

Deirdre English

My God is now sex.

Linda Lovelace

People who are fascinated with sex and make it their god are repressing religion.

Alan Watts

Sexuality has ceased to be equated with warmth and tenderness. It's become a "thing" that has to be done . . . We describe loving with four-letter words.
Dr. Leo Buscaglia

Procreation's rituals are described in the Tantras. They include adoration of the genitals as images of the divine principles poised to unite to accomplish the miracle.
Alain Daniélou

Somewhere in their mounting and mating, rutting and butting is the very secret of nature itself.
Graham Swift

Love must conquer the old matter of sex and reveal the new, in which the union of man and woman will mean not the loss but the realization of virginity, i.e., of wholeness. It is only from this fiery point that the transfiguration of the world can begin.
Nicholas Berdyayev

There is tremendous importance in the action of sexual passion. Governed by God, mixed with benevolence, sweetened by the spirit of heaven, it is productive of unbounded happiness and improvement.
J. H. Noyes

Sexual pleasure, wisely used and not abused, may prove the stimulus and liberator of our finest and most exalted activities.
Havelock Ellis

Why do we try to intellectualize sex anyway? (Just) realize at that moment you are at the pleasurable epicenter of the Milky Way galaxy.

Dennis Miller

To be inspired means to be "in spirit." When you are inspired, very often you are making love to the person that you adore.

Dr. Wayne Dyer

Lord, love me hard, love me long and often. I call you, burning with desire. Your burning love enflames me constantly. I am but a naked soul, and you, inside it, are a richly adorned guest.

Mechtild of Magdeburg

Only by satisfying the need for physical love will it be possible to guarantee the development of the noble element in love.

Charles Fourier

Sex is a sacrament: the outward and visible sign of an inward and spiritual grace, bringing about love.

Alan Watts

I think we can't go around measuring our goodness by what we deny ourselves. I think we have to measure our goodness by what we embrace.

JoAnne Harris, in "Chocolat"

Refrain from suppressing natural urges. Any suppression of our physical natures causes an inner reaction, a kind of distortion that destroys inner harmony.

Nik Douglas and Penny Slinger

By giving yourself to any beautiful sensation,
however small, you more than double it – every
time you touch good and enjoy it, you touch God;
and there are infinite depths there, however small
the surface may appear.

J. H. Noyes

Sex is a celebration of life!

John-Paul Sousa

Sexuality is an expression of our spirituality.

Pamela Anderson

There is only one temple in the world, and that is
the human body. Nothing is holier than this high
form. One touches heaven when one touches a
human body.

Novalis

There are no lower passions. We require a new
conception of the sanctity of these things. What we
have despised and dishonored are sacred things,
and they must be restored to the honor which is
their due.

John S. Bayne

Eroticism is firstly a search for pleasure, and the
goal of techniques of love is to attain the divine
state, which is infinite delight.

The Kama Sutra

We pray that the young men and young women of
today and tomorrow will grow up with the

realization that sex is a beautiful flame they carry in the lantern of their bodies.

Demetrius Manousos

The net result of the sexual experience is that you begin to understand God.

Deepak Chopra

Lord, give me chastity and continence, but not yet.

Saint Augustine

The sexual embrace can only be compared with music and with prayer.

Havelock Ellis

₌17₌

Screwy Sex Laws

• An Hawaiian law makes it illegal to appear in public wearing only a swimsuit.

• A San Antonio, Texas law makes it illegal for men or women to flirt or respond to flirting using either their eyes or hands.

• An ordinance in Miami makes it illegal for a man to wear any kind of strapless gown.

• It is illegal to bathe in Oregon unless you wear clothing that covers you from the neck to the knee.

• In Pacific Grove, California, molesting a butterfly carries a $500 fine.

• Hartford, Connecticut law forbids a man from kissing his wife on Sunday.

• Men who deflower virgins in Auburn, Washington are subject to five years in jail.

• In Schulter, Oklahoma it is against the law for any woman to gamble in the nude, in lingerie, or wearing a towel.

• Halethorpe, Maryland makes it illegal to kiss for more than one second.

• In Eureka, Nevada, it is illegal for men with moustaches to kiss women.

• A St. Louis law prohibits a firefighter from rescuing a woman who is wearing a nightgown. She must dress first in order to be rescued.

• A Charlotte, North Carolina law requires women to be covered in at least 16 yards of clothing at all times.

• A San Francisco law makes it illegal to wipe your car with used underwear.

• People who flirt on the streets of Little Rock, Arkansas are subject to a 30-day jail term.

• Kentucky makes it illegal to remarry the same man four times.

• A Clawson, Michigan law makes it illegal for a farmer to sleep with his pigs, cows, horses, goats, and chickens.

• Seattle makes it a crime punishable by six months in jail for a woman on a bus or train to sit on a man's lap without a pillow between them.

• An ordinance left on the books for years in Los Angeles permits a man to beat his wife with a leather strap, provided the strap is less than two inches wide, or the wife gives permission to use a wider strap.

• Morrisville, Pennsylvania requires women to obtain a permit in order to wear cosmetics.

• Wisconsin has outlawed kissing on a train.

• In Salem, Massachusetts, it's illegal for even married couples to sleep naked in a rented room.

• Dyersburg, Tennessee makes it illegal for a woman to call a man for a date.

• A New York City ordinance forbids a man on the street from turning around and looking at a woman "in that way." Violators can be required to wear horse blinders.

• Hornytown, North Carolina has a law banning all massage parlors.

• Portland, Maine makes it illegal for a man to tickle a woman under the chin with a feather duster.

• North Carolina law requires couples staying in hotels must stay in double beds which are a minimum of two feet apart. Loophole seekers beware: having sex on the floor between the beds is also strictly illegal.

• Under Kentucky law, it is illegal for a female to wear a bathing suit on a highway unless she is accompanied by two police officers, or armed with a club, or weighs less than 90 pounds or more than 200. Female horses are exempt, however.

• In Cleveland, Ohio, it's illegal for women to wear patent leather shoes because reflections of their underwear might be seen by men.

• A Monroe, Utah law requires that daylight be visible at all times between couples on a dance floor.

• Columbus, Georgia law prohibits anyone sitting on a front porch in an indecent position.

• Tulsa, Oklahoma outlaws kisses lasting over three minutes.

• Oxford, Ohio makes it illegal for a woman to undress in front of a picture of a man.

• New York City makes it illegal for a woman to appear in public wearing body-hugging clothing.

• Georgia law makes it illegal to change a store mannequin's clothes unless the shades are drawn.

• It is illegal to have sex in a church yard in North Carolina.

• A Raton, New Mexico ordinance outlaws a woman wearing a kimono from riding horseback down a public street.

• A Chicago ordinance prohibits taking a French poodle to the opera.

• A Detroit ordinance makes it illegal to have sex in a car unless it is parked on your property.

=18=

Screwy Place=Names

Authentic place-names in Great Britain:

Aspull, Bitch Burn, Broadbottom, Butt Green, Chicklade, Cockermouth, Holeopen Bay West, Laide, Laytown, Little Cocklick, Long Load, Maidenhead, Penistone, Peterhead, Pishill, The River Suck, Titley.

Authentic place-names in America:

Alabama
Ballplay, Chigger Hill, Pulltight, and Smut Eye

Arizona
Hookers Hot Springs

Arkansas
Toad Suck, Toilette, Blue Ball, Pansy, Weiner,
Ben-Gay, and Needmore

Colorado
Hygiene

Connecticut
Laysville

Delaware
Ogletown

Florida
Dildo Key

Idaho
Dickshooter

Illinois
Wacker

Indiana
Hooker Corner

Kansas
Studley

Kentucky
Knob Lick

Louisiana
Dry Prong

Maryland
Chewsville and Crapo

Michigan
Buttman

Mississippi
Big Bogue Homo

Missouri
Tightwad

Nebraska
Colon, Wynot, and Wymore

New Hampshire
Chickville and Sandwich

New Jersey
Dicktown

New York
Sodom and Puckerville

North Carolina
Hornytown, Bushy, Erect,
Boogertown, Bottom,
Leatherman, and Climax

North Dakota
Dickey and Flasher

Ohio
Footville and Tightwee

Oregon
Pee

Pennsylvania
Virgin, Lickingville, Intercourse, Hop Bottom,
Pithole, Lover, and Husband

Texas
Ding Dong

Utah
Hardup and Virgin

Virginia
Assawoman and Tight Squeeze

Washington
Humptulips

Wisconsin
Hustler and Spread Eagle

Wyoming
Groin

꞊19꞊

Resources

Get involved! Our rights as individuals depend on the willingness of people to defend them. Protect your right to discuss, read, view, hear, and possess what others would like to censor.

ORGANIZATIONS

Adult Industry Medical (AIM)
(*Founded by former porn star Sharon Mitchell, AIM's purpose is to provide counseling, support, and medical testing to people in the adult entertainment industry.*)
14241 Ventura Boulevard, #105
Sherman Oaks, CA 91423
(818) 981-3851 or (818) 981-5681
www.aim-med.org

American Civil Liberties Union (ACLU)
125 Broad Street, 18th Floor
NY, NY 10004-2400
(212) 549-2500
www.aclu.org

Free Speech Coalition
Because freedom isn't free
Box 10480
Canoga Park, CA 91309
(800) 845-8503
www.freespeechcoalition.com

Fans of Adult Entertainment (FOXE)
*(Founded by Bill Margold, FOXE gives fans and porn
stars a chance to meet at a variety of events, from charity
softball games and auctions to an annual FOXE Awards
dinner/dance.)*
8033 Sunset Boulevard, #851
Los Angeles, CA 90046
(723) 656-6545

National Coalition Against Censorship
*(A group that monitors attempts at censorship and reports
them on their website.)*
275 Seventh Avenue
NY, NY 10001
(212) 807-6222
www.ncac.org

Protecting Adult Welfare (PAW)
They've been your best friends, now you can be theirs
*(Also founded by Bill Margold, a 30 year veteran of the X-
rated industry and author of The Porn Stud Handbook.
PAW prides itself on providing a realistic view of the pros
and cons of working in the sex business, along with
counseling for those entering or leaving the industry.)*

4523 Van Nuys Boulevard, #205
Los Angeles, CA 91403
800-506-4999
www.pawfoundation.org

BROTHELS

Nevada is currently the only state in the United States to allow legalized prostitution in designated areas. (Las Vegas is not one of them.) Like any other business, new brothels open and others close. For a complete listing of brothels in Nevada go to www.nvbrothels.com.

The Moonlite Bunny Ranch
(One of the oldest and most famous brothels in Nevada. They pioneered the concept of bringing in porn stars for special guest appearances and close encounters with fans.)
30 Moonlight Road
Mound House, NV 89706
(888) BUN-NYRA
www.nvbrothels.com/mlbr.htm

BOOKS, NEWSPAPERS, MAGAZINES

Adult Video News
(This magazine covers the adult entertainment industry and related First Amendment issues.)
9414 Eton Avenue
Chatsworth, CA 91311
(818) 786-4286
www.avn.com

Eden Press
(Publishers and distributors of books about personal freedom, privacy and financial independence.)
Box 8410
Fountain Valley, CA 92728
(800) 338 – 8484
www.edenpress.com

Lana Holstein, MD
(Nationally-known expert on sexuality. Director of Women's Health at Canyon Ranch Health Resort in Tucson, Arizona. Assistant Clinical Professor at the University of Arizona School of Medicine. Dr. Holstein is the author of "How to Have Magnificent Sex: The 7 Dimensions of a Vital Sexual Connection." She's also featured in the video "Magnificent Lovemaking," which was broadcast on public television stations.)
www.lanaholsteinmd.com

Screw
(The self-described "World's Greatest Newspaper" was founded by Al Goldstein in 1968. Since then it's been fighting the good fight against sexual and political hypocrisy, while advocating sexual openness.)
43 W. 24th Street
NY, NY 10010
www.screwmag.com

Spectator Magazine
(This publication covers sexual openness, alternative lifestyles and free speech issues.)
Box 1984
Berkeley, CA 94701
(510) 849-1615
www.spectator.net

Video Xcitement
(This newspaper covers the amateur and professional adult entertainment industry with product reviews and news of events.)
Box 187
Fraser, MI 48026
(313) 463-1347
www.videoxcitement.com

CLOTHING AND NOVELTIES

Adam & Eve
For cheerfully consenting adults
(Sellers of sex toys, love lotions, sexy outfits, CD-ROMs, condoms.)
Box 800
Carrboro, NC 27510
(800) 293-4654
www.adameve.com

Frederick's of Hollywood
(The original merchant of erotic wear.)
6608 Hollywood Boulevard
Hollywood, CA 90028
(800) 323-9525
www.fredericks.com

Lady Calston
We don't just sell toys, we make them!
(Daryl Brown, a sexy mother of five, started this company with one sex toy: a vibrating tongue. Calston now offers a full line of erotic toys and clothing.)
1051 Clinton Street, Suite 204
Buffalo, NY 14206
(800) 690-5239
www.calstoncyberstore.com

Miko Exoticwear
A women run store
(A source for shoes, boots, lingerie and gifts with a sexy attitude.)
653 North Main Street
Providence, RI 02903
(401) 421-6646
www.mikoexoticwear.com

Playmates of Hollywood
(Designers and sellers of fun nurse, firefighter, etc. sexual fantasy outfits.)
6438 Hollywood Boulevard
Hollywood, CA 90028
(888) 464-7636
www.playmatesofhollywood.com

Very Intimate Pleasures (VIP)
(Suppliers of exotic dancewear, theme outfits, g-strings, swimsuits, club wear, and body glitter.)
100 Brainard Road
Hartford, CT
www.viphartford.com

Victoria's Secret
(Famous for their catalogs and stores of sensuous lingerie.)
Box 16589
Columbus, OH 43216-6589
(800) 888-8200
www.victoriassecret.com

VACATIONS

Hedonism Resorts
Be wicked for a week
(Choose from Hedonism II or Hedonism III for the
vacation of a lifetime. You'll find yourself in a lush
tropical setting with other fun-loving adults. Singles and
couples are welcome. Outdoor sex and free love are
encouraged, but not required.)
(877) 467-8737 or (954) 925-0925
www.hedonismresorts.com

The Lifestyle Organization
For playful couples who love the erotic part of being
adults
(This group holds annual swingers' conventions and
clothing-optional getaways.)
2641 W. La Palma Avenue, Suite F
Anaheim, CA 92801
(714) 821-9953
www.lifestyles.org

VIDEOS

Anabolic Video
(Producers and distributors of inter-racial, world, and
group sex videos and DVDs.)
534 Victoria Avenue, #3
Venice, CA 90291
(800) 326-2789 or (310) 827-1257
www.anabolic.com

Arrow Productions
(Specialists in classic adult videos from the 1970s to the present.)
631 Las Vegas Boulevard
Las Vegas, NV 89101
(800) 762-4624
www.deepthroat.com

Excalibur Films
(A complete selection of videos and DVDs from all producers. Their fan-friendly website lets you search for your favorite XXX stars and gives you performer bios and photos.)
3621 W. Commonwealth
Fullerton, CA 92633
(800) Buy-Movies or (714) 773-5855
www.excaliburfilms.com

Extreme Video
(Producers of popular oral, anal, and fetish videos.)
16140 Leadwell Street
Van Nuys, CA 91406
(818) 779-6479
www.extremeassociates.com

Femme Productions
(Candida Royalle's erotic videos created for couples to enjoy together. More romantic and less graphic than most.)
Box 268
NY, NY 10012
(800) 456-LOVE or (212) 979-5988
www.royalle.com

Max Hardcore

(*Proceed with caution. Max has a style all his own.*)
www.maxhardcore.com

Homegrown Video

(*Men and women from around the country send Homegrown their private sex videos for your viewing pleasure.*)
Box 420820
San Diego, CA 92142
(858) 541-0280
www.homegrownvideo.com

Hustler

(*Larry Flynt's line of videos, DVDs, and magazines.*)
8484 Wilshire Boulevard, #900
Beverly Hills, CA 90211
(877) 325-6464
www.shophustler.com

JM Productions

(*Producers of intense and off-beat videos.*)
9018 Balboa, #576
Northridge, CA 91324
(818) 348-1256
www.jerkofzone.com

Rodney Moore

(*If you like seeing average office workers and college students go at it in imaginative little vignettes, you'll probably enjoy Rodney's line of videos.*)
3435 Ocean Park Boulevard, #112
Santa Monica, CA 90405
www.rodneymoore.com

Ed Powers

(*Ed has a unique ability to talk average girls-next-door into performing sex for his line of videos. He also hosts his own radio show every Saturday night on KLSX 97.1 in Los Angeles.*)
421 N. Rodeo Drive, #15247
Beverly Hills, CA 90210
www.edpowers.com

Price Busters

(*Low prices on videos, DVDs, magazines, and sex toys.*)
Box 28130
Las Vegas, NV 89126
(800) 223-8244
www.pricebusters.com

Private International

(*Arguably, the most beautifully produced porn in the world can be found in Private and Pirate videos and magazines. They celebrate sexuality in lush outdoor settings around the world, featuring healthy, gorgeous men and women – mostly from Europe or South America – who actually seem to be enjoying themselves!*)
P.S.I.
Apdo 30.035
08080 Barcelona
Spain

P.S.I. Group
Box 17079
104 62 Stockholm
Sweden

Odyssey Group (Private Representative in US)
Box 77597
Los Angeles, CA 90007
(800) 369-6214
www.private.com

The Sinclair Intimacy Institute
Great lovers are made, not born
(Producers of Better Sex Advanced Techniques
instructional video series.)
Box 8865
Chapel Hill, NC 27515
(800) 955-0888
www.bettersex.com

Video Alternatives
(Producers of spirituality/sexuality instructional material
and distributors of amateur adult sex videos.)
14 Burgundy Drive
Lake St. Louis, MO 63367
(800) 944-1902
www.videoalt.com or
www.understandthesystem.com

Printed in the United States
17301LVS00002B/81

9 781401 047399